ELECTRONIC SHORTHAND

ELECTRONIC SHORTHAND

AN EASY-TO-LEARN METHOD OF RAPID DIGITAL NOTE-TAKING

MICHELLE CAMPBELL-SCOTT

Coo Farm Press

Electronic Shorthand: An easy-to-learn method of rapid digital note-taking

US edition. First printing November 2016

ISBN-13: 978-1539552208

ISBN-10: 1539552209

This book is for you if you are...

- A reporter or trainee reporter;
- A student of any kind – real world or online;
- A business person;
- Someone who make lists – to do lists, shopping lists, books to buy, etc;
- Someone who takes notes while watching online videos or webinars;
- A lifelong learner.

It will enable you to take notes quickly and accurately on a device (smartphone, tablet, laptop, or computer). The notes will be fairly confidential as you will have made up your own abbreviations for many words. They will be easy to read back in the future (even decades into the future). They will also be available across multiple devices and operating systems and therefore easy to retrieve in different situations.

If you already know shorthand or speedwriting, you will still find this useful as neither shorthand nor speedwriting transfer well to an electronic environment.

This method is not ...

- A new language;
- Difficult – you will pick it up straightaway and build on it as you use it in everyday life;
- Something that will take you hours and hours of study;
- A waste of your time – you will use it in all sorts of situations.

In loving memory of Muriel Chisholm,
whose grandchildren's pencil cases were
always the best-stocked

CONTENTS

PART THREE – SPEEDING UP

INTRODUCTION

THE 18TH CENTURY British author Charles Dickens, like his character 'David Copperfield', chose to learn a method of shorthand in order to improve his career prospects. His new skill enabled Dickens to become a Parliamentary reporter.

He studied shorthand from a '10-shilling shorthand manual'[1]. 10 shillings is equivalent to about $500 today so the book in your hands is quite a bargain!

Whether or not you have aspirations of becoming a reporter –the reporters I know love this method - you probably need to take notes occasionally.

We often think we are going to be able to remember something but generally our memories let us down,

---

1 Source: http://www.lrb.co.uk/v30/n23/leah-price/diary

unless we have done memory training. Notes are really important if you don't have an eidetic memory.

They're also important for fact-verification, legal matters, and anything that you need to refer to with 100% accuracy at a later date.

Students in particular are known for note-taking – or rather they used to be. It's common now for teachers and professors to give out their notes and PowerPoint presentations to their classes. This has led to a decline not only in note-taking but in the ability of students to take notes.

Yet research shows note-taking is very valuable. One study[2] showed that students who took notes performed better than those who didn't. The students who took notes averaged 72% correct answers, whereas the students who didn't averaged 61%. That's a full grade difference.

Most students would be very glad of the opportunity to improve their exam scores by a full grade. Forward-thinking schools and colleges do teach note-taking skills but, unfortunately, they teach pen & paper based methods. To the Googling generation!

Then they wonder why the kids 'don't get it'. If they taught electronic methods they might have more success.

Notes are great if you can actually manage to get everything down that you want **and** read it afterwards. For many people, that's just not possible. Illegible notes

---

[2] 'A note-restructuring intervention increases students' exam scores. Cohen, D.; Kim, e.; Tan, j.; & Winkelmes, M. (2013)

and a sore hand are pretty normal for most students and many business people, too.

I was fortunate to learn Pitman shorthand while in school (I wanted to be a reporter and thought it would come in useful) and never forgot it. I've used it while taking notes in business meetings, trainings, seminars, workshops, online training courses, while watching YouTube videos, webinars, sermons, and more.

I've never been a company secretary or the designated person for taking the notes but I have a poor memory (as a result of a knock on the head in a car wreck) and notes really help. So I take notes wherever I go and whatever I'm doing. They sometimes turn out to be very helpful and have even proved useful for me legally.

I have taught High School and been a business trainer. Both places contained people who needed to take notes, write quickly and legibly, and be able to find those notes and read them back afterwards – often months or years afterwards. The students in school needed their notes for learning, revision, and homework.[3] The business people needed them for various purposes: taking client briefs; product knowledge; telephone messages; training sessions.

Most of the students in school and the business people in my seminars and workshops took notes by hand – pen and pad. Writing notes out by hand is a tedious, inefficient, and sometimes painful process. Even if you

---

[3] And to help them stay awake in boring lessons! The hand(s) movement of note-taking helps the brain stay engaged.

can write reasonably quickly, you can't hope to match the speed of someone speaking, and you will miss lots of what is said.

If you have any type of problems with your hands or fingers, you may struggle to grip a pen for any length of time. Some conditions, such as dyslexia and dyspraxia, result in problems with holding a pen as well.

So what's the alternative? One that works for some people is traditional shorthand. It enables you to write faster than people speak[4] – up to 200 words per minute (wpm) - and is great if you have the time to learn it and don't have problems writing or holding a pen.

Shorthand systems, like other languages, take many hours of study and practice. The popular Teeline system today takes a minimum of 40 hours of study (not including practice), larger systems such as Gregg take longer. Teeline became popular because reporters discovered that it is quicker to learn than other forms of shorthand such as Gregg and Pitman.

Not everyone wants to write out their notes with pen and paper, especially now that we tend to store our whole lives on gadgets such as smartphones and tablets. Typing, for many people, is much quicker than writing – even on a fiddly smartphone! Writing notes with pen and paper means you either end up with a lot of bits of paper or you have to type them up or scan them into a computer eventually.

One of the big problems with traditional methods of shorthand is that it can't be done on a gadget or

---

4 People speak between 110 and 160wpm.

computer. They are composed of various types of squiggles that don't transfer to a computer because there aren't the keys for them!

There are numerous methods of traditional shorthand. They're all composed of squiggles but vary greatly. They do have a few things in common with each other, though. They:

- Take many hours of study to learn – followed by months of practice;
- Can only be done with pen and paper;
- Are supposed to be taken while sitting down with a pad on a table.

Speedwriting[5] is a more modern version of shorthand. It uses the alphabet and resembles the texting language which is familiar to many of us. One of the drawbacks of shorthand is that you really need lined notepaper to write it properly - otherwise it can be difficult to read back consistently. Lined notepaper isn't always available. Speedwriting doesn't require lines and can be scribbled on the back of an envelope and still be read/understood properly. You can't achieve the same speeds as you can with shorthand but it's an immensely useful option for people who don't want to learn a whole new language.

The trouble is that pen and paper methods seem pretty obsolete. So traditional shorthand methods aren't relevant today for those of us who never have a pen but

---

[5] A system of Speedwriting was invented in the 20s in Chicago by Emma Dearborn, who taught at the university. She used many of the abbreviations that people who use text language on cellphones would recognize.

always have an electronic device! There may be keyboards composed of the shorthand squiggles but, as they'd only be suitable for typing shorthand, you would have to switch keyboards to do other work – which would get irritating pretty quickly!

I was a few months off buying my own iPad when I saw one being used in a business networking meeting. The lady was an HR professional and was in the training seminar before lunch. She took lots of notes on her iPad and I chatted to her about it afterwards.

She explained that she found it much more useful than writing on bits of paper, which could get lost or creased, and which needed to be typed up afterwards for permanent storage. The iPad gave her the ability to do the work once and store it in the cloud[6] for later search and retrieval.

One of the people I was teaching at the time was a Medical Secretary who had to take fast, accurate notes on a laptop in multi-disciplinary team meetings. Thoughts and ideas were batted backwards and forwards and she needed to be able to get it all down very quickly and then knock it into shape afterwards. It was quite scary for her, because her notes were broadcast live onto a screen on the wall for everyone to see as she took them. She often fumbled over the keys and found it extremely stressful and difficult – to the point where it was affecting her health.

---

[6] Storing things online is known as storing them in 'the cloud'. Services for this include: Dropbox, OneDrive, iCloud, GoogleDrive, etc.

I wanted to help her and tried using various verisons of speedwriting on a computer myself so I could show her how to use that on her laptop. None transferred well because some of the abbreviations in speedwriting can only be done by hand and others create words that are too open to interpretation to be used reliably by people needing to use their notes in important business environments.

To use one version of speedwriting[7] on a computer you would need to take the time to convert some of the letters into superscript and subscript, which would take too long to be considered a quick way of taking notes.

For example, a subscript 's' represents the 'sh' sound and a subscript 'c' represents the 'ch' sound. So you might write:

$\mathbf{S}_s$ for sash, or

${}_c\mathbf{K}$ for check

To do that you would need to type the letters in full first, then highlight one letter and make it subscript (or superscript). That's far too fiddly and overly time-consuming – especially on a smartphone or tablet (if it is even possible, I'm not sure!).

It needed some thought and experimentation. I investigated the limited number of computer-based note-taking systems and, for various reasons, rejected them.

[7] The system by Heather Baker, which is excellent.

Some were very complicated and difficult to use – which meant many hours of study and time putting it into practice. Others were very expensive. People who need to take notes **now** don't have the time or inclination to learn an entire new language. They need something quick and easy to pick up. They aren't always professional secretaries or PAs, they can be people from all walks of life – who just don't want to learn a completely new language.

I continued to experiment and develop my own system, based on the principles but not the squiggles of traditional shorthand. Over a period of two years, I refined and settled on just a few easy lessons and guidelines. That's what you have in your hands, my method of electronic shorthand.

My typing speed is 120wpm – as fast as I got with Pitman shorthand back in High School. My electronic shorthand speed is based on my typing speed. Actually faster than my typing speed, as I'm typing that fast while using abbreviations! Everyone I have taught this method to has found that their note-taking speed improves week after week, as does their typing speed. I suggest you combine your learning of electronic shorthand with learning how to type properly and quickly. It makes a huge difference. See the Getting Faster chapter.

The lessons in this book are easy to learn, quick to implement, and simple to transcribe into 'real' writing in Word or another word processor. Transcribing isn't always necessary, though, because notes taken in this system of electronic shorthand can be read back just as they are, months or even years later.

I found the system very helpful myself and wondered if it would transfer to smartphones and tablets. I often take notes on my iPhone. It's handy because it's always with me and I can take notes wherever I am – even standing up – and they automatically sync to the cloud so are available on my computer when I get home.

I tweaked my system a bit more and found it sped up my note-taking to the extent that I can get down ***most*** regular speech (e.g. in meetings that don't get particularly heated!) word-for-word. Sometimes people naturally speak very quickly but even then I don't have to leave much out.

Like at least a third of the population, I'm a kinesthetic learner. That means I don't understand well if something is explained (which auditory learners prefer) or shown (which visual learners prefer). I need to do, feel, and experience in order to understand things – and, especially, to remember them.

Kinesthetic learners don't do well if we have to sit and listen. If I am in a seminar or conference, because I'm not an auditory learner, there is a real danger of me switching off mentally or falling asleep. I need to ***move*** or I can't concentrate. Taking notes helps keep me awake, helps me understand what is being said/taught, and enables me to process and remember much more than if I don't take notes.

Kinesthetic learners aren't the only ones to benefit from note-taking though. The act of taking notes helps with understanding and retention of the subject-matter.

I have found that electronic shorthand reduces the stress levels of people who learn it because they can use their notes as reminders and task lists and don't have to worry about not remembering something, it is easy to refer back to.

Lots of people have studied this method[8] and found it immensely useful. I hope you do too.

So how can electronic shorthand help you? Fewer people are learning shorthand today, yet secretaries still exist and still need to take notes and minutes. Many people have to attend business meetings and training sessions and need to jot down points and reminders. You can do that with pen and paper, sure, but the chances of being able to find that piece of paper in six months when you need it are pretty remote – considering all the other bits of paper that seem to fill our lives.

Digital notes are different. They don't need typing up afterwards, they are searchable if you want to find a certain point, they are easy to retrieve, they are fairly confidential as few people will be able to understand them (that won't include you if you learn the main principles in this book!), and you can add security so other people can't even open them.

Learning this new skill could help you with any studying you do, in your business/work, and in your hobbies. It can make note-taking faster and more fun

8 In real-world and online classes.

and hopefully relieve you of some stress. It is good to know that your notes are stored safely and are easy to find and search when you need them.

Imagine taking notes on an iPhone during a visit to a doctor. Then, years later, going to a different doctor in another country, who doesn't have access to your medical records. You could bring up your notes from the earlier meeting – even if you have swapped phones numerous times in the intervening years, because you stored your notes in an online service such as Evernote – and explain when you last had that illness and what the doctor prescribed for it. These are the sorts of things we routinely forget. Not anymore!

This method also transfers to pen and paper, which is something people appreciate when their smartphone batteries die! Once you have learned this method, you can also use it when writing notes the old-fashioned way.

About This Book

This book is split into four easy lessons but you don't need to do them all at once – in fact that isn't a good idea. You will learn better if you start slowly, just with the first lesson, and start using your new skill straightaway so you get lots of practice. Then you can go on to learn more, which will speed up your note-taking and encourage you to continue! You just need to invest a bit of time and get to know the principles of each lesson well, before starting to use them all together.

Ideally, give yourself a week to get used to each lesson. That will ensure that it has become second-nature and you won't struggle to remember what you learned last time while trying to implement what you learned this time! If you are a particularly quick learner then of course you may choose to move through the lessons more quickly – that's fine, just don't put unnecessary pressure on yourself.

You can start incorporating your own abbreviations early on. These will vary depending on why you are taking the notes. You may work in a medical field and have certain things you write over and over. Some people like to take notes in seminars, meetings, or religious services. Again, there will be repeated phrases and abbreviations. I'll show you how to incorporate these into your note-taking as we go through.

Let's start with a look at some safety things first ...

~ PART ONE ~

The Groundwork

HOW NOT TO END UP IN HORRIBLE PAIN

"Safety is something that happens between your ears, not something you hold in your hands."

~ Jeff Cooper

A FEW YEARS back, I got quite ill with headaches that wiped me out for days. They were accompanied by severe neck pain that was so bad I could only get some relief by lying down. It was like my neck could no longer hold my head up.

My [adult] son came into my office one day and, after staring at me, said he knew what was causing my head and neck pain. I was working on a laptop and he noticed that my head was tilted down at an unnatural angle. He ordered me a laptop stand/riser and it arrived the next day (good service from Staples in the UK!). I started using it straightaway and my headaches stopped the following day. I couldn't believe how simple – and quick - the solution was.

You would think I would have learned from that but I recently did it again! Once I started working from home as a writer I switched to a desktop computer and forgot about my experience with head and neck problems when using a laptop as I used one so infrequently.

On vacation recently I only had a laptop with me and used it a lot to Skype with family back home, write blog posts, and do some studying. I ended up at a chiropractor's office, in such pain that they rushed me in without an appointment.

It was a different type of pain, coming from the muscle on the right side of my neck at the back. It radiated up over the top of my head. Again, I was only able to get some relief when lying down. The chiropractor fixed it and advised cold packs and rest. It didn't come back, as I had finally learned the lesson!

If you do overdo it, I highly recommend going for a chiropractic checkup.

CHIROPRACTOR'S NECK STRAIN TIP

Soak a towel in cold water, wring it out, then pop the twisted towel in the freezer.

Half an hour later, or when you need it, take it out and lie down with it under the back of your neck. It will give your neck pressure and support on the painful areas and soothe it with coolness, reducing inflammation.

You could also end up with hand and wrist pain from overuse and improper posture. Pain can travel up the arms even to the shoulders.

Simple pain is bad enough but if it gets worse it could be Repetitive Strain Injury (RSI). RSI is a painful and debilitating condition caused by repeated movement. If you start taking lots of notes at speed, you could suffer from it if you don't take a few precautions.

Maintaining Good Posture & Hand Positioning

Prevention is always better than cure so remember these four simple things to maintain good posture and hand positioning:

1. Your neck should have a curve[9]. Put one hand on it and, if it feels straight, you are probably leaning forwards;
2. Feet should be flat on the floor. Not crossed, not propped up. I'm only 5' 4" and a lot of seats are too high for me so I like to put my feet on a block of wood or a small toolbox to get my thighs parallel;
3. Hands and arms should be parallel with the floor (or desk);
4. Eyes should be looking straight ahead, preferably with the top of the screen at eye level.

---

[9] Chiropractor Dr John Bergman has lots of excellent (free) videos on YouTube about the importance of keeping a good curve in your neck.

Try to ensure that you maintain good posture and hand positioning whenever you take notes. What may start off as a two-minute note while standing in line for coffee can turn into a full-blown article when you take the coffee to a table - still hunched over your smartphone.

Bear in mind that any time you take notes (whether at a computer or on a device), you need to keep your head up so you don't get neck ache. Hold your device higher if you find yourself leaning forwards and take regular breaks from looking down at it.

Hand positioning is very important. When at a computer or laptop, many of us develop bad habits. Check your hands frequently to make sure they are level with your lower arms, which need to be parallel with the desk. Any tilting of your hands will cause problems eventually.

If you type frequently on smartphones, you will need to ensure that you take regular breaks. Flex and spread your fingers out at least every ten minutes. It may seem fussy, but you could be saving yourself a lot of pain and frustration in the future if you take these simple precautions.

One of the problems I had was in holding my phone. I developed a nasty habit of holding it in my right hand with my pinky extended underneath the bottom of it to hold it steady while I typed. I developed pain in my pinky that radiated up my palm and wrist.

The older phones were worse, as many of them were smaller than the big smartphones that are popular now. This meant our thumbs were at odd, unnatural angles and caused a lot of thumb RSI. Thumbs weren't designed to operate at that angle.

Be careful when holding a smartphone or tablet.

You may be holding your neck awkwardly or sticking out a finger at a weird angle.

Both of these habits can cause long-term damage and a variety of odd symptoms.

Stretching & Exercises

Human bodies were designed to move. It is totally unnatural to do what many of us do all day – sit still at a desk. When sitting, our digestion and blood circulation slow down, we tend to hunch forward and straighten our important neck curve, and we can get sluggish mentally.

When siting down, it's important to get up at least once an hour to walk around. If you can't – I imagine air traffic controllers are restricted from wandering around! – try doing some exercises at your desk. It's that important.

If you can take breaks, the ideal is every 20 minutes. Go for a glass of water, use the bathroom, stroll to take a note to a colleague rather than email.

I work mostly from home, so I schedule household tasks into my work breaks: first break of the day I put a load of washing on; second I hang it out to dry or put it in the dryer; third I do some stretches on my gymball.

There are great hand and wrist exercises at this page:

http://www.stretchnow.com.au/resources/exercises/hands-exercise

And some really useful back exercises at this page:

http://www.stretchnow.com.au/resources/exercises/back-exercise

Perfect posture/position isn't always possible so try to work for short periods and take regular 'stretch' breaks. Go for a walk, roll your shoulders, flex and stretch your fingers, ease your neck back. Your future self will thank you!

Now you're going to do this without injuring yourself, let's jump in to learn some of the lessons we can take from old-fashioned shorthand methods ...

~ GETTING STARTED ~

Some Shorthand Basics

WHEN YOU HAVE studied something for a while, it affects your thinking, and your life in general. So it was with shorthand, for me.

I've done a lot of study over the years, as well as sat in many business meetings. I find myself, when writing with pen and paper, throwing in the odd Pitman shorthand word or abbreviation. It's just second nature to me, as I spent years learning and practicing it in my teens.

I can only do that when writing with a pen though. When typing on a computer or smartphone, the only bits of shorthand I used were some of the abbreviations I had learned all those years ago. Some abbreviations transfer to a computer, some don't.

I used:

- 'f' for 'if'
- 'v' 'of'
- 'ng' for 'thing'
- 'b' for 'be'
- 'r' for 'are'
- A 'g' added to the end of any word to represent 'ing'

This worked and I worked with simple abbreviations for years at my computer.

When I eventually came up with my method of electronic shorthand, I decided to base it on a lot of it on the traditional shorthand principles – because they work. Those are to:

- Write using the sound of words rather than how they are spelled;
- Write outlines of words rather than full words;
- Base outlines on consonants;
- Only add vowels that are absolutely essential to understanding;
- Combine words and use abbreviations whenever possible.

These principles form the basis of electronic shorthand. When you start using the abbreviations I suggest, you will actually be using old shorthand abbreviations that have been around for centuries – which is pretty cool considering the fact that you'll be using them on an electronic device!

In old-fasioned shorthand, words are comprised of 'outlines' (consonants) joined together to make words, with dots and dashes added to them to represent vowels.

That sort of shorthand requires you to learn an entire new language of shapes for letters. We don't need to learn a new language in electronic shorthand. Every letter we type only requires one click on the keyboard, whereas writing some letter shapes such as 't' requires two movements of the hand. So we're ahead already!

Then the deeper traditional shorthand students go into their learning, the more vowels they leave out until eventually they hardly write any at all. Traditional shorthand only keeps in vowels that are absolutely essential to the understanding of the word.

Many vowels can be left out because a lot of words written just in consonants can be understood.

For example:

shrthnd

bnkrpt

So that's the background of electronic shorthand. It will seem very familiar if you have ever either read or sent a text - in text language - on a cellphone. It will be quick to learn, which is great for confidence. Mastering a new skill makes us feel good!

Let's jump into the first lesson ...

~ PART TWO ~

The Lessons

~ LESSON ONE ~

Using outlines

ONE BIG THING the different systems of shorthand and speedwriting have in common is a rule to base most words on consonant 'outlines' and leave out certain vowels. This is similar to the 'text' language that some people use with cell phones.

For example:

Cn u rd ths?

translates as:

Can you read this?

Simple enough if you have ever read a text - but what if it got a little more complicated?

See if you can work out the following verses of poetry, which are written in basic text language:

Gv m ur trd, ur pr, ur hddld msss yrnng to brth fr. Th wrtchd rfs f ur tmng shr.

Snd ths, th hmls, tmpst-tssd t m, I lft my lmp bsd the gldn dr!

Btfl drmr, wk nt m, Strlt & dw drps r wtng for the; snds f the rd wrld hrd in th day, Luld by the mnlt, hv all psd awy.

Did you get them? The full verses are in Appendix 2. Some people can decipher them, some can't. Not to worry, because the difficulty with this is my point.

Many people can decipher basic text language but it can get confusing and complicated because we often need to know which vowels are being missed out. 'trd' could be 'tread', 'tired', or 'turd', for example!

When we read words in the context of the whole sentence – especially when it is a familiar verse - we can usually work out the correct meaning, as in the 'can you read this' example. But we won't always be reading familiar verses. Some words won't be in complete sentences and we need to be sure we will be able to read them back accurately – especially if we need to take important notes, such as for legal or medical purposes.

In English, as in many other languages, vowel letters can have different sounds. When a vowel sounds like its ***name*** it has a long sound.

For example:

a is pronounced ***ay***

e is pronounced ***eee***

i is pronounced ***eye***

o is pronounced ***oh***

u is pronounced ***yoo***

We are going to use vowels that have long sounds and leave out vowels that have short sounds.

Leaving out short vowels is simple to remember and if you say the word to yourself in your head you can 'hear' if it has a long or a short sound.

For example:

The long ***eee*** sound in ***bead***

The short ***e*** sound in ***bed***

The method we will use is simple: we will only be adding vowels of a certain type. So that, if a word outline has a vowel, we know how it will sound – it will be a long sound.

This handling of vowels is important and will stop us getting mixed up with:

tm – team or time?

rd – read or red?

nd - need or nod?

Long Vowels

Have a look at these words, all of which have *some* long vowels.

ape	**feel**	**pie**	**over**
name	**me**	**white**	**cute**
bee	**these**	**close**	**huge**
even	**lie**	**home**	**prune**

We need to keep in the long vowels in those words but we can remove short vowels and also any duplicated vowels – apart from initial vowels (which we'll look at later on).

So they would look like this:

ap	**fel**	**pi**	**ovr**
nam	**me**	**whit**	**cut**
be	**thes**	**clos**	**hug**
evn	**li**	**hom**	**prun**

If we read them back, they should read just like they did in the earlier version, even though we have removed some letters.

That's because we know that **if there is a vowel in a word it is a long sound**.

Short Vowels

These words all contain short vowels.

apple	**bed**	**in**	**God**
bag	**hen**	**zip**	**bus**
yam	**wet**	**cot**	**under**
mad	**bin**	**pop**	**run**

Here's how they look with the short vowels removed:

apl	**bd**	**in**	**Gd**
bg	**hn**	**zp**	**bs**
ym	**wt**	**ct**	**undr**
md	**bn**	**pp**	**rn**

Could you read them okay? Bear in mind that we will be reading back our electronic shorthand in context with other words in the sentence and it is easier to read a whole sentence than individual words.

With all that in mind, what do you think these sentences say? If you read them aloud, quickly, you should be able to tell.

Th ct st on th mt redng a not & etng an apl

Th bg bd wlf scard ltl rd ridng hd

Red ths rd book wil I wat

I've capitalized the long vowels in the full sentences below and underlined short and silent vowels to show which were removed.

The cat sat on the mat rEading a nOte & Eating an apple

The big bad wolf scAred little red rIding hood

REad this red book whIle I wAit

The longer a word is, the more letters you can leave out. You can leave out almost all the vowels from long words – except any initial vowels.

Some words are so long that you can leave out lots of letters, often the entire ending.

Take this unusually long word...

Llanfairpwllgwyngyllgogerychwyrndrobwlll lantysiliogogogoch

It is the longest place name in the U.K., a village on the Welsh island of Anglesey. It is one of the longest words in the world, containing 51 letters. The locals just call it...

Llanfair pg

(pronounced Lan-fair-P-G[10])

It's a great example of a word that you can really abbreviate and still understand!

[10] By non-Welsh speakers! Welsh people pronounce LL like a combination of H and L.

In fact, if you Google just *Llanfair pg* you should get results for the place.

Pronouncing & Spelling Vowels

You already know how to pronounce vowels but it's a good idea to try to forget how they look and should be spelled. Instead, think about how they **sound**.

For example:

The 'oh' sound in 'goad' can be written 'o' = ***god***

The 'oo' sound in 'good' can be written 'u' = ***gud***

It makes it much clearer to read back. You aren't wondering whether it's boat or boot.

This leads us to the way different nationalities and regions pronounce words. If any words in this book use a different sound spelling, change it to one that fits with your pronounciation.

Your Own Abbreviations

The words and abbreviations you use will depend on why and where you are taking notes. You will probably start to drop even some long vowels from words you use frequently.

For example, if you take notes in religious services you could use **gd** to mean **God**, and you could use **gud** for **good**. In a lecture (other than one on theology!), the use of the word God would be rare, so it might make more sense to use **gd** for **good**.

Any words that you are likely to use frequently should be abbreviated as much as possible, and you'll need to build up your own personal dictionary of electronic shorthand words and abbreviations.

One of the advantages of using this method is that your notes will be unique to you. Other people learning this system would stand a good chance of reading some of them back, but not all of them, as you will use many of your own abbreviations. This makes your notes quite secure, as notes written in shorthand of old were always considered to be.

You can use a simple notebook or Word document for this, or download the free template I have prepared at the following URL:

http://www.digitalnotetaking.org/ worddictionary

CHALLENGE

Start thinking about the SOUND of words, rather than the spelling.
We'll look more at this later in the book.

Exercises

1. Put a check in the column 'Short' or 'Long' to indicate whether you think it is a short or long sounding vowel. The answers to these and all the other exercises in the book are at the back, in Appendix Two.

WORD	SHORT	LONG
need		
shop		
stay		
mad		
made		
lock		

There will be some words that you have to think about more than others, so it is good to do some practice to get you in the swing of things.

2. Write out these abbreviated words in full. Speak them out loud, quite quickly and they should make sense:

wl	
wul	
ht	
hat	
bled	
tak	
lok	
gd	
metng	

Great. Next, we'll write them the other way around – from English into electronic shorthand.

3. Write the abbreviated words as best you can:

little	
better	
handsome	
pretty	
beep	
beat	

4. Try deciphering these song titles:

Jny b gud	
Gud vibratns	
Rspct	
Smls lik ten sprt	

Vowel Deliberations

In electronic shorthand, as in traditional shorthand, we can sometimes even leave long vowels out safely, if the word is:

- ***Long*** – the more letters there are in a word, the less chance there is of confusing it with another word.
- Part of a ***sentence*** – we can easily guess a word when it is accompanied by other words.
  For example, 'need' should be **ned** because it has a long 'ee' sound. 'nd' could be 'nid' or 'nod'. However, when used in a sentence, it becomes obvious that the word should be 'need'.
  I nd u 2 ...

More Examples

Let's look at writing some opening lines from books in electronic shorthand. If you can, type these out on a device or computer, so your fingers get used to the new outlines.

It was the best of times, it was the worst of times.[11]

[11] From *A Tale of Two Cities*, Charles Dickens

This is quite an easy one. Here's how it could be written:

It ws th bst f tims, it ws th wrst f times.

But let's hone it down some more. 'f' is a traditional shorthand abbreviation for 'if'. 'v'is the abbreviation for 'of'. So we'll stick to that.

More on specific abbreviations later but this is a good one to start with. So it will now look like this:

It ws th bst v tims, it ws th wrst v times.

Okay, onto the next book opener:

It was a bright cold day in April, and the clocks were striking thirteen.[12]

This could become:

It ws a brit cld dy in Apr, & th clks wr strikng 13.

Some explanation here. The first few words are obvious – 'brit' is an easy contraction for 'bright', and 'dy'for 'day' is another good abbreviation that you can add to your repertoire.

I have used 'Apr' as it is a pretty standard abbreviation for 'April', as is '&' for 'and'.

'clks' can't really be mixed up with another word – unless we are writing about chickens and calling them 'clucks'! – so it is a handy contraction.

12 From *1984*, George Orwell

'wr' for 'were' is another one you can add to your electronic shorthand dictionary as it's a handy abbreviation. We'll use a variation of it for 'where' later on.

I am a sick man ... I am a spiteful man.[13]

This could become:

I am a sk mn ... I am a spitfl mn.

Not much to take out here. 'sk' is good for 'sick' as it reads like that when you speak it out. 'spitfl' works well for 'spiteful', because it has a long 'i'.

You may decide to us 'm' for 'am'. I don't, as I use 'm' for 'me' but each to their own!

Great, that's it for this first lesson. We've made a good start. Or ... **wev mad a gud strt!**

[13] *From Notes from Underground,* Fyodor Dostoyevsky

RECAP & ACTIVITY

Practice taking notes by typing outlines, using what you now know:

- Write words using outlines mainly made up of consonants
- Leave out short vowels
- Keep in long vowels

Try to practice your electronic shorthand by taking notes whenever you can: while watching TV; while streaming a YouTube video. You probably won't get everything that's said (people speak very quickly sometimes!) but jot down as much as you can.

As you progress through the book and learn more techniques and abbreviations as your note-taking will speed up tremendously. Comparing how much detail you can get down later on to how much you got down now will be very encouraging.

The more you use your new abbreviations, the more your brain will make new neural pathways, making them easier and easier to use and remember.

Don't worry about speed or accuracy at this stage. Once you are used to deciding which vowels to leave in, go on to the next chapter.

~ LESSON TWO ~

Handling initial & end vowels

INITIAL VOWELS REALLY help our understanding when reading back electronic shorthand. They are super important.

There are occasions when we won't use them though and that's when we will use commonly-abbreviated words. For now, concentrate on keeping in initial vowels and don't worry about speed, as we will be more than making up for adding a few initial vowels as you work through this book.

The following words really miss their initial vowels:

lrm

tlty

tm

nct

They are supposed to be:

alarm

utility

item

enact

But you can't tell that from the electronic shorthand words above that didn't use their initial vowels.

They would read back much better with those initial vowels:

alrm

utlty

itm

enct

So bear that in mind when taking notes and you should be able to read your electronic shorthand back easily.

End Vowels

We need to keep *most* end vowels. The following words would be very hard to read back if their end vowels were missing:

yucca

khaki

jujitsu

Writing 'yucca' as 'yc' (as the 'u' has a short vowel sound) just doesn't make sense. But if we keep in the end vowels they are easy to understand:

yucca = yca

khaki = kki

jujitsu = jjtsu

There's an easy way to remember which end vowels we need to keep – everything except E.

If a word ends with A, I, O, or U, keep the end vowel. End vowels help because we can often leave more letters out if there is an end vowel, as it aids our understanding of the word.

Here are a few examples:

llama = lama

zoo = zu

corgi = crgi

tikka = tka

gelato = glato

graffiti = grfti

yeti = yti

feta = fta

gecko = gko

broccoli = brcli

pizza = pza

hippo = hpo

FOCUS ON E

If a word ends in 'e' it usually has a long vowel sound. We don't usually need to keep 'e' at the end of words:

note = not

acute = acut

apple = apl

Words don't change their meaning by not having an 'e' at the end. We do, however, need to keep 'e' if it appears at the beginning of a word. For example:

eat = et

ewe = ew

each = ech

They really wouldn't work without the initial 'e'.

Exercises

What do the following sentences say?

1.

Th alrm rng erly @ th zu

2.

Jak th gko is blu

3.

An apl ech dy kps the doc awy

4.

Th ew at th pza

Now write out the electronic shorthand for the following.

5.

Oh, Danny Boy, the pipes, the pipes are calling from glen to glen, and down the mountain side.

6.

There is nothing either good or bad, but thinking makes it so.[14]

7.

Now is the time for all good men to come to the aid of the party.

8.

The corgi rode the llama into the palace.

[14] From *Hamlet*, by William Shakespeare.

RECAP

Practice taking notes using what you now know, focusing on:

- Writing words made up mainly of consonants
- Leaving out short vowels
- Keeping in long vowels
- Keeping initial vowels
- Keeping ***most*** end vowels apart from 'e'

Again, use whatever opportunities you can to practice your note-taking. TV, YouTube videos, radio, meetings, etc., are all great sources of free dictation materials.

Don't worry about speed or accuracy ... yet!

Once you are used to keeping initial vowels and most end vowels apart from 'e', go on to the next chapter.

~

That's it for this lesson. A nice short one that is easy to implement. I suggest you practice as much as possible before continuing to the next lesson.

~ LESSON THREE ~

Write What You Hear

IN THIS LESSON we are going to focus on the ***sounds*** of words. A lot of English words are unnecessarily complicated and we can miss out a lot of letters and speed up our electronic shorthand.

If you were an alien just landed and starting to learn to write, then you would probably spell words more phonetically. Little children do this all the time.

For example:

External – you would probably write **xternal**

The word is still readable without the initial 'e' because the 'x' actually has the sound of 'ex'. Most words were written as they sounded prior to the 15th century. As they sounded differently to different people, the same word could have multiple different spellings in common use. Shakespeare famously used various spellings of his own name!

Then French and Latin words were introduced, as printing presses started to be used and words became more complicated and more precise.

Over the years, as people move about various countries and trends change, pronunciation tends to change. But spelling doesn't. So we have ended up with some quite antiquated ways of spelling words.

Around 60% of words in English have silent letters. Letters that we can easily leave out of our shorthand and yet still leave the meaning intact. This is very handy for us - by doing this you will be writing about 60% faster!

Silent Letters Save Us Time

When taking notes it is hard to think up new ways of spelling words, in accordance with the electronic shorthand rules. That's why we work them out in advance, and put together our own dictionaries.

You'll no doubt be aware of tons of silent letters once you read the following but may not be able to bring any to mind at a moment's notice if you were to try (same here!).

W – e.g. written = **rtn**, wrap = **rp**

B after **M** at end of word – e.g. crumb = **crm**

B before **T** – e.g. debt = **dt**

C when with **scle** – e.g. muscle = **msl**

P when before **H** – e.g. telephone = **tlfon**

As we know, **E** at the end of a word – e.g. note = **not**

D in the middle of a word (not always – not 'middle') – e.g. handkerchief = **hnkrchf**

G before **N** – eg. sign = **sin**

GH suffix – e.g. thought = **thrt**, light = **lit**

K before **N** – e.g. knife = **nif**, knee = **ne**, knock = **nk**

N after **M** suffix – e.g. hymn = **hm**

S before **I** – e.g. island = **ilnd**

U after **G** – e.g. guest = **gst**

Words From Other Countries

Some letters are silent in Scandinavian words but only for their English versions! They pronounce the 'k' in knife in Sweden (kneefe).

Viking words such as 'gnat' used to be pronounced as they are written but now we don't say the 'g'.

'h' is silent in words of French origin. For example, 'hour' has a silent 'h' but 'hotel' doesn't – 'hour' is taken from French.

If English is your mother tongue, you probably won't be able to drop initial Hs though. So most of us would write 'hr' for hour and that's fine.

'gh' is silent in some words of Anglo-Saxon origin, in two ways:

- When used in the middle of a word. For example, 'daughter', which we could write as **drtr**.
- When used at the end of a word. In this case, it has a 'ff' sound. For example, 'enough'. We can substitute an 'f' for the end 'gh'. For example 'enough' could be written as **enuf**.

This may all sound rather complicated, and a lot to remember. It really isn't. When you start concentrating on writing only what you ***hear***, you will automatically leave out silent letters.

Doing this is good for us as it wakes up parts of our brains that are usually dormant. We tend to write according to how we were trained in school, how we know things should be written. This is new and different, and it is good for us! It makes us think in new ways, ways that our brains aren't used to.

So, don't worry about it, just be aware that lots of letters are silent. When you come across them in your note-taking, know that you can safely leave them out without losing the ability to read your notes back. Your brain will do the rest.

Spotlight on Phonetics

You already know how to pronounce words, of course, but let's think about how to use them in a much more phonetic (how words sound) way in our note-taking.

A word here about specific regional and cultural variations. I'm from the UK and there are regions that drop the word 'the' – it becomes just a 't', as in:

T'bird in t'hand = the bird in the hand

(a popular pub name in Yorkshire)

Shop on t'corner = Shop on the corner

(the actual name of a shop in Lancashire)

And some regions drop the 't' completely from the middle of certain words:

compu'er = computer
wa'er = water

(this is a London thing that is popular among some young people throughout the UK!)

Even if a word or letter isn't generally pronounced in your region, it may be easier to choose to include it in your electronic shorthand. It's up to you, of course, but in my experience, people find it easier for legibility.

You can, however, come up with your own electronic shorthand abbreviations based on your region or particular way of speaking. That will make your notes less easier to read by others so makes them more confidential!

G & J

G can sound hard (guh), as in **go** (**g**) or soft (juh), as in **large** (**lrj**). When the sound is soft, write a J.

Hard G examples:

grasp = grsp

gave = gav

Soft J examples:

wreckage = rkj

gem = jm

judge = jj

'judge' is an example of a silent D – drop those too!

W

It's fairly easy to drop silent Ws from note-taking. Start typing 'write' as 'rit' and you will see what I mean.

Examples:

It is wrong to write on the wall = It is rng 2 rit on the wal

Wrath of Khan = Rth v Khan

Wreck It Ralf = Rk it Rlf

There are instances where you may drop an 'ew' as it has a 'yoo' sound. This helps distinguish it from similar words too. For example:

new = nu

If we wrote it as nw, it could be 'now'.

C & K

C often has a soft sound – as in **ace** - and K always has a hard sound – as in **kite**.

When 'c' is used with 'k' (usually in one-syllable words), pronunciation is a hard 'kay' sound. That is so that people don't sound is as an 's' sound! You don't need the 'k' to guess the pronunciation of a one-syllable word such as 'crack' but if 'crac' became 'cracing', you might sound is as 'crasing' if it didn't have the 'k', because 'c' is often soft when it's surrounded by vowels. So in electronic shorthand we will shorten 'crack' to **crk**.

Way back, 'k' was actually added to many more words alongside 'c' – such as 'musick', and 'publick' – but that stopped over time as it's uncessary.

When C is used at the start of a word, the sound is generally hard – so we'll use a K there. (In Latin, C had a sound of either K or G so this is much more simple than that!)

We'll use:

- C for a soft 'cee' sound – e.g.:

  place = place   cease = ces

- K for a hard 'kay' sound – e.g:

  placate = plkat   crease = kres

If you type a 'c' in a word you know it's a soft sound. You never need the 'c' when there's a combination 'ck'. As in 'wreckage' (**rkj**), earlier, simply drop the initial 'c', because it is silent anyway.

F & V

We have already started using **v** for **of** and **f** for **if**.

F has a soft 'eff' sound and V has a hard 'vee' sound. F sounds also occur in words with 'ugh' in them as well as words with 'ph'. So we can use:

laugh = lf

enough = enuf[15]

graph = grf

photograph = fotgrf[16]

[15] This is an example of an instance where you would throw in a short vowel, to aid understanding. There isn't a word 'enoof! **Enuf** is one of my abbreviations but you may prefer **nuf** or **enf**.

[16] If this was 'photo' you would add the second 'o' (**foto**) as end vowels are important for understanding (apart from E). In 'photograph', though, it becomes unnecessary, because the longer a word is, the more vowels you can leave out.

S & Z

Use S when it is a soft 'ess' or 'sss' sound and Z when it is a harder 'zzz' or 'zuz' sound.

For this reason, I prefer certain American spellings of words over English spellings. I think it must be far easier for people who are learning English! The Z in 'realize' makes sense, the S in 'realise' doesn't.

said = sd

soft = sft

says = sz

realize = realize or realz

I generally find I can drop a long vowel before a 'zuz' sound because you speak it anway.

Don't worry if you don't take to all of this right away. You will ease into it over time.

I dropped initial 'w's almost immediately but it took me quite a while to drop 'gh's from my electronic shorthand. I'm making far more use of 'zuz' sounds than I used to as well.

When taking notes, I often make up new abbreviations on the spot and so do my students. They look for new words to shorten and add to their personal abbreviation dictionaries.

Exercises

Try deciphering these lines:

1.

My drtrs dns s gd enuf

2.

Dd u rit th crd & rp th prznt?

3.

Uz th nif in ur rit hnd

4.

Th gsts at th htl thrt th nu sin ws lvly

Now try writing the electronic shorthand for these lines:

5.

Call me crazy, but I love you

6.

Singing hymns on the island

7.

Your handkerchief is in the wash

8.

I have a cough and a cold

RECAP

Practice taking notes using what you now know, focusing on:

- Skipping silent letters
- Writing letters as they sound, rather than as they are generally spelled (e.g. large = lrj)
- Use C for words that have Cs with soft 'ess' sounds
- Use K in words that have Cs with hard 'kay' sounds
- Use F instead of gh or ph
- Use Z in place of S when it is a harder 'zzz' or 'zuz' sound

This lesson may be a little more difficult to implement as you won't be used to thinking about the sounds of words.

As always, grab any opportunities you can to practice your note-taking. You may notice that your speed is starting to increase a little at times but then stalls at others as you try to remember what to write – that's normal!

The more you write electronic shorthand, the more naturally it will come to you and the faster you will type.

~ LESSON FOUR ~

Use Abbreviations

IN CLASSES WHERE I have taught electronic shorthand, I ask people to call out abbreviations that they use in everyday life, so I can write them on a flipchart. As always happens when we're are asked to come up with something, the mind first goes completely blank - it's as if we've never heard an abbreviation in our whole life! That's perfectly normal.

When people think about it for a while, though, most start to remember a few abbreviations. In classes one or two people will call out a couple of abbreviations, saying that's all they use. When others in the group give their abbreviations, though, everyone else will usually say, "Oh, yes, I'd forgotten about that one, I use that all the time".

We do use abbreviations a lot but we are so used to using them that we can actually forget that they are abbreviations.

There are the obvious ones such as:

eg (for example)

etc (etcetera)

asap (as soon as possible)

cont/d (continued)

gov (government)

demo (demonstration)

but there are many, many more in everyday use. More importantly, there are lots more that we can make up and make them part of our personal dictionary of abbreviations.

The abbreviations you choose will tend to be for the words you use most often in your note-taking. That will probably be influenced by the industry you work in, the fields you study, or the hobbies you do.

Try to think about some of the abbreviations you use in everyday life and then some of the ones that you use in your work or study. No matter how many you can come up with now, if you come back to your list in a day or two, you will probably be able to add more.

For this reason, I am going to suggest some of the most commonly-abbreviated words so you can start to use them. You will probably want to come up with your own later on, when you have a more complete list of the ones you use frequently.

Start using standard abbreviations in your note-taking. Use symbols whenever you can, they save a lot of time and speed up your writing. For example, using **%** saves using a lot of letters.

Also use numerals instead of words, not just to represent numbers. For example, 2 can represent to, too, or two. 4 represents for or four.

Some Abbreviations To Start With

We have already started using some abbreviations:

v = of　　**u** = you

As well as numerals:

2 = to/two　　**4** = for/four

Let's expand that now with a few more:

g = go　　**f** = if

t = it　　**s** = is

imp = important　　**m** = me

Use standard abbreviations and numerals to begin with

You may prefer to use M for 'am' rather than 'me'. It comes down to personal preference. In traditional shorthand, the symbol for 'me' is an M, as is the symbol for 'am'. Where it is written on the line determines whether it is 'me' or 'am'. So, when I switched to electronic shorthand, I had to decide which to use M for and went for 'me' as a quick search through my documents showed that I type 'me' far more than 'am'.

What do these sentences say:

1.

f u g 2 th c, t s cld

2.

t s imp 2 g strat acrs

USING SYMBOLS

Check the symbols on your keyboard (or in the alternative keyboards on a device). There are lots to choose from.

You could use the currency symbol as an abbreviation for 'money'.

% is obvious, and in everyday use, as are @ and #. The trouble is, when we hear someone say 'percentage' our finger reaches for the 'p' key, not the '5' key; we hear 'number' and we start typing an 'n', not the '#' key. That's why determining which symbols you are going to use and practicing them is so important.

Add the ones you feel you would remember to your electronic shorthand dictionary and start to use some of them in your note-taking.

How about using the star symbol on the '8' key to mean a long word that you use in everyday note-taking, such as the name of your company or a long word that you can't usually spell?!

If you're still a 'hunt & peck' typist, you may not find symbols easy to incorporate into your note-taking. It's worth spending a bit of time practicing symbols in whatever typing tutor program you use. They really do save a lot of time. Typing '%' is much, much quicker than typing 'percentage'!

If you are on a device, you need need to click something else before you can access the alternative keyboard(s) where the numerals and symbols hang out. On my iPhone, I have to hit the '123' key, then the symbols key to get to the symbols. If a symbol isn't going to save you multiple keystrokes, it isn't worth using.

So percentage (%) and number (#) are worth it, @ for 'at' isn't. Perhaps you could use @ for 'another' or something else.

A WORD ABOUT 'SO'

I've chosen 's' to represent 'is' rather than 'so' because 'is' is used more frequently in English.

However, 'so' is used a lot in the spoken word. Speakers often say it at the start of a sentence in such a way that it is completely meaningless. I'm often horrified when listening to myself on recordings, I say it way too often!

When taking notes, be aware of this fact. You can safely leave out many instances of 'so' – especially if they occur at the beginning of a sentence.

Bear in mind that you may chose different abbreviations, mine are just things that work for me.

Specialist Abbreviations

There are lots more abbreviations that may not be familiar to you. They vary in different industries – medicine is known for using a lot. You can see why, when you see the length of some of the disease names!

Take a look at these medical abbreviations that I have used in everyday, non-medical note-taking:

BP = blood pressure	**DC** = discontinue/discharge
Px = prescription	**Bx** = biopsy
c/o = complains of	**DC** = description
dc = discontinue	**Dx** = diagnosis
dist = distilled	**ext** = external
inj = injection	**liq** = liquid
stat = immediately	**ss** = a half

The field of mathematics uses a lot too:

< = greater than
> = less than
/ = divided
x = multiple(ied)
= = equals
+ = plus/add
arg = argument
corr = correlation
def = define
grad = gradient
int = interior
LHS = left-hand side
min = minimum
max = maximum

As does the computer industry:

cat = category
MC = multiple choice
DB = database
MB = megabyte
DL = download
HA = high availability
HD = high density
tmp = temporary

And chemistry. If you know the periodic table, it could save you a bit of time in your note-taking if you have to type any chemical names.

Ag = silver
Al = aluminum
Au = gold
C = carbon
Mg = magnesium
Na = sodium
O = oxygen
Zn = zinc

CO_2 = carbon dioxide[17]   **CO** = carbon monoxide

You can borrow as many abbreviations as you want from specialist industries. I write on health, so use plenty of medical abbreviations. I used to be an IT teacher, so I also incorporate plenty of computer industry abbreviations.

If you want to learn some more abbreviations, go to:

WWW.ABBREVIATIONS.COM

There are thousands on there. Choose a few that fit with your field of work or study and add them to your personal electronic shorthand dictionary. Also try to select ones that you think you will remember!

I use abbreviations because I know them. If you aren't familiar with abbreviations and try to use them, they will actually slow you down at first as you struggle to remember them! It is worth persevering though, as they will save you lots of time eventually. As always, just learn a few at a time and practice incorporating those into your note-taking before learning new ones.

[17] Word will probably autocorrect CO2 to CO_2. On a smartphone or tablet, don't worry about trying to make the '2' subscript because CO2 could not mean anything else in your notes.

Using Capitals

Capitals can be used to represent whole words or even phrases. You can come up with your own capital letter abbreviations – starting with just one or two until you get used to them – or use some or all of mine.

The best thing to do is come up with your capital letter abbreviation list – or use of my list - over a period of time.

As you read back your electronic shorthand you will notice which longer words come up most often, and you can choose capital letters to represent those words.

Here are mine:

O = only **K**= thousand

M = multi **T**= thing

U = under

You may choose to add more, for example:

A = another **B** = beautiful

C – century/country **D** = difficuilt/difference

E = every **N** = tion/tian

You can use capital abbreviations on their own or as part of other words. For example:

1A = one another **10K** = 10,000

MNl = multinational

They're a good way of saving a lot of time when typing.

I have included more of my abbreviations in the next chapter. Pick and choose the ones that you feel you would remember and start incorporating them a few at a time into your note-taking.

Exercises

What do these sentences say?

3.

ps m th 2x4 blk

4.

the cst s $1K

5.

any1 els bt u

6.

sh wrks hrd 4 th $

7.

f th % v ppl @ th evnt s sml, u wl nt mak enuf $

8.

th ptnts BP s > 150 so h nds a Px & an inj

9.

th liq ws M-us

Now type these sentences out in electronic shorthand:

10.

The five people in the top percentage of the class all came from the same country

11.

Moneywise is another very different multinational company

12.

The difference between carbon monoxide and carbon dioxide is small but very important

13.

Government cutbacks caused demonstrations in the streets

14.

Problems arose when the number of tickets sold was greater than the number of seats available

RECAP

Okay that was the last lesson! Here's what we covered:

- Use common abbreviations as much as possible in your note-taking
- Use symbols to represent whole words – if you're on a device, though, only do this for long words (e.g. 2 instead of 'to' won't save any time as you have to hit the CAPS key)
- Learn new abbreviations and start adding one or two at a time to your electronic shorthand dictionary

If you continually add new abbreviations to your working collection and you will find that your writing speeds up tremendously. Abbreviations save us so much time.

Later in the book you'll find ways to customize Word to turn your abbreviations into full words.

The next chapter contains extra exercises where you're going to read some harder examples of electronic shorthand. Try typing these out to see which you like, so you can add them to your own collection.

EXTRA EXERCISES

Lines from classic books

1.

Prid rlats mor 2 r opnn v orslvs; vnty 2 wt w wld hv othrs thnk v us.

2.

Al hpy fmls r alik; ech unhpy fmly s unhpy n es own wy.

3.

T ws a quer, sltry smr, th smr thy elctrctd th Rosenbergs, & I ddn't knw wt I ws dng n NY.

4.

n th lat smr v tt yr w lvd n a ho n a vlj tt lkd acrs th rvr & th plan 2 th montns.

5.

**Shl I cmpar the 2 a smr's dy?
Thou art mor lvly & mor tmprat**

6.

**Lik as th wavs mak 2wrds th pbld shor,
so d our mins hstn 2 thr end,
ech chnjg plac wv tt wch gs b4,
n sequent toil al 4wrds d cntnd.**

7.

U wl rej 2 her tt no dsstr hs acmpnd th cmncmnt v an entrpris wch u hv rgrdd wv sch evl forbodngs.

8.

Mr Hungerton, hr fthr, rly ws th mst tctls prsn upn erth.

9.

Th yr 1866 ws sgnlsd by a rmrkbl incdnt, a mystrus & pzlng phnmnn, which dbtls n1 hs yt frgtn.

Lines from the Bible

10.

n th begg, Gd creatd th hvns & th erth.

11.

Th hvns dclar th glry v Gd.

12.

4 I knw th plns I hv 4 u, dclars th Lrd. Plns 2 prspr u & nt 2 hrm u, plns 2 gv u hop & a fut.

13.

I cn d al Ts thru Ch wh strnthns m.

Lines from famous speeches

14.

I hv a drem tt 1 dy ths ntn wl riz up & lv ot th tru meng v es cred: "W hld thez trths 2 b slf-evdnt: tt al mn r creatd =."

Mrtn Lthr Kng

15.

Ask nt wt ur cntry cn d 4 u, ask wt u cn d 4 ur cntry.

J.F. Kndy

16.

I kp my ideals, bec n spit v evT I stl bel tt ppl r rly gud @ hrt.

An Frnk

17.

Tt gov v th ppl, by th ppl, 4 th ppl, shl nt prsh frm th erth.

Gtysbrg Addr

18.

Nvr n th fld v hmn cnflct ws so mch owd by so mny 2 so fw.

Wnstn Chrchl

19.

W shl dfnd our ilnd, wtevr th cst ma b. W shl fit on th bechs, w shl fit on the lndng grnds, w shl fit n the flds & n the strts, w shl fit n the hls; w shl nvr surr.

Wnstn Chrchl

20.

Frnds, Rmns, cntrymn, lnd m ur ears.

Shksper

21.

4 fols rsh n whr angls fer 2 trd.

Alxndr Pop

22.

4tun fvrs the bld.

Virgil

23.

Drem as f u'l lv 4evr, lv as f ul di 2moro.

Jms Den

24.

Nvr dwt tt a sml grp v thrtfl, cmtd ctzns cn chnj th wrld. Inded, t s th O T tt evr hs.

Mrgrt Med

Quotes from politicians

25.

I am nt a crok. I hv ernd evT I hv gt.

Rchrd Nxn

26.

Th O T w hv 2 fer s fer itslf.

Frnkln Dlano Rzvlt

27.

Poltcl ldrs stl thnk Ts cn b dn thru 4c, bt tt cnt slv trorsm. Bkwrdns s th bredg ground v tror, & tt s wt w hv 2 fit.

Mkhal Grbchv

28.

t s ez 2 mak prmss – t s hrd wrk 2 kp thm.

Brs Jnsn

29.

Ther r no dsstrs, O opps. &, inded, opps 4 frsh dsstrs.

Brs Jnsn

30.

Lik Indiana Jons, I dnt like snaks – tho tt mit led sm 2 ask y im n pltcs.

Thresa Ma

SUGGESTED ELECTRONIC SHORTHAND DICTIONARY

Here is my electronic shorthand dictionary. I have put all my favorite contractions and abbreviations into my Word AutoCorrect dictionary so that I can type away in electronic shorthand, secure in the knowledge that Word is correcting my contractions and abbreviations into full English. It's pretty cool!

Bear in mind that I have been doing this for years so I have built up quite a collection. I incorporated abbreviations a few at a time though. I'm not a quick learner and I don't like to overwhelm my memory!

Traditional shorthand is very big on abbreviations. I studied both Gregg and Teeline after learning Pitman but went back to Pitman as I preferred it. What I did learn from Gregg, though, was to use almost every letter of the alphabet on its own to represent a word. Gregg is very big on abbreviations.

Abbreviations are essential if you want to get really fast in your note-taking. In shorthand, there is a phenomenon known as the 80wpm plateau. That's the speed students reach and get stuck at. Until they start incorporating lots of abbreviations into their repertoire, they stay stuck at 80wpm. Once they start using abbreviations, though, they jump to 100, 120wpm and more.

Some of these abbreviations are very close to old shorthand or speedwriting abbreviations but I've abandoned those that don't transfer well to a keyboard. I also ignored any that can be misinterpreted. In the original 1923 speedwriting manual, there were a lot of words that were so contracted that they read like other words. For example, **mon** = more than. But in electronic shorthand we would read mon as moon. So we don't use that. If you use 'more than' a lot, though, you could create your own abbreviation. Perhaps **Mn** or **mthn** or the 'greater than' symbol (**>**).

Use abbreviations whenever you can to speed up your writing but be sure to get used to just a couple of new shorthand abbreviations before learning more.

Try to get lots of practice of note-taking so that your fingers do the work and you don't have to think too hard!

FULL WORD	COMMON &/OR ELECTRONIC SHORTHAND ABBREVIATION
A	
abbreviation	abbr
about	abt
action	actn
address	addr
additional	addl
afternoon	pm
alternate	alt
and	&
and so on	etc
anything	anyT
approximately	aprx
are	r
around	arnd
as long as	ala
as soon as possible	asap
association	assn
at	@
author	auth
available	avlbl
avenue	ave

B

b	be
because	bec
before	b4 or bef
before noon	am
beginning	begg
belief	belf
believe	bel
between	bet or btwn
body mass index	BMI
business	bsns
business to business	B2B
business to consumer	B2C

C

call-to-action	CTA
can	cn or kn
captain	capt
carbon dioxide	CO2
care of	c/o
cat	ct
Celsius	C
change	chnj
changed / changing	chnjd / chnjg
character	char
charge	chrj
college	clj

come	cm
company	co
computer-aided design	CAD
copyright	(c)
corporal / corporation	corp / corpn
correct	crct
could	cd
county	co
couple	cpl
crowd	crwd
crowd-funding	cdfdg

D

dear	dr
deep vein thrombosis	DVT
degree	deg
department	dept
detail	det
develop	dev
difference	difc
different	dif
difficult	dift
direct / direction	dir / dirn
disease / diseases	dsz / dszs
district	dist
doctor	doc
document	dcmt

do	d
dog	dg
doing	dng
dollar	$
done	dn
don't know	DK
doubt	dwt
down	dwn

E

east	E
easy / easiest	ez / ezt
easier / easily	ezr / ezly
economy	ecny
education	educ
effective	efctv
efficient	efcnt
equal / equals	= / =s
equal to	=2
especially	esp
establish	est
everything	evT
example / for example	eg / 4eg
experience	exp
experienced	expd
experiment	expm
external	extl

extraordinary	exord

F

family / families	fmy / fmls
fast / faster	fst / fstr
favor	favr
fiction	fctn
finally	fnly
first	1st
focus	fcs
follow / followers	folo / folors
for example	eg
for/four	4
fortune	4tun
forward	4wd
foundation	fndtn
frequently asked questions	FAQ
future	fut

G

general	gen
generally	gnly
general practitioner	GP
genuine	jnin
given	gvn
go	g
God	gd
going	gg

good	gud
goodness	gdns
governor / government	gov/govn
graduate / graduated	grad/gradd
greater than	>
ground	grnd
group	grp
great	grt
guarantee	guar
guaranteed	guard

H

happen / happening	hpn / hpng
happy	hpy
have	hv
headache	hdach
height	ht
hour	hr
house	ho
how	hw

I

identity/identify	ID
if	f
I'm	im
in	n
increase	incr or ^

increasing	incrg or ^g
information	info
institute	inst
interest / interesting	int / intg
Internet Service Provider	ISP
internal	intl
is	s
it	t
it is	es

J

jambalaya	jmblya
job	jb
journey	jrny
judge	jj
judgement	jjmt
junior	jr

K

kangaroo	kngro
keep / keeping	kp / kpg
key performance indicators	KPI
king	kng
knowledge	nlj or knlj

L

laboratory	lab
language	lang
large	lrj
leader	ldr
leads to	leds 2/->
learn / learning	lrn / lrng
less than	<
limited	ltd
little	ltl
local area network	LAN

M

massage	msaj
maximum	max
may	ma
message	msj
meter	M
migraine	migran
minimum	min
minus	-
minute	min
money	$ (your currency)
more	mor
mount	mt
mountain	mwntn
mouse	mws

much	mch
museum	mus

N

negative	neg
north	N
not available	n/a
not equal	n/e
nothing	nT
novel	nvl
number	#

O

occasion / occasional	occn / occl
of	v
offer / offered	ofr / ofrd
only	0
opinion	opnn
opportunity	opp
opposite	oppt
ordinary	ord
original / originally	orgl / orgly
out	ot
over / overcome	ovr / ovrcm

P

page	pj
part	pt
parliament	parl
percentage	%
plus	+
population	pop
positive	pos
pound	lb (or £)
problem	prob
programme	prog
progress	prgrs
public relations	PR
publish / publisher	pub / pubr
publishing	pubg

Q

qualification	qualtn
quality	qualty
quarantine	quartn
queen	qwn
question	Q
quick / quickly	qwk / qwky

R

radiation	radtn
raise/rise	rz

reading	rdg
reader	rdr
reading	rdg
realize	rlz
recover	rcvr
reference	ref
register / registered	reg / regd
regular / regularly	reg / regly
research & development	R&D

S

sacrifice	sac
saint	St
second	2nd
see/sea	c
service	svc
some	sm
somebody	smbdy
something	smT
sometimes	smtms
south	S
street	st
subject	subj
subtract	subt
suceed	scd
succeeded	scdd
surrender / surrendered	surr / surrd

T

thank you	TY
that is	ie
their	thr
there	ther
therefore	th4
they're/they are	thyr
thing	T
though	tho
thought	thrt
times or multiply	x
to/too/two	2
trademark	TM
travel	trvl

U

ultimate	ult
uncomfortable	uncbl
under	U
understand / understanding	Ud / Udg
unique	uniq
unique selling point (or proposition)	USP
university	uni
unpublished	unpubd

V

value	valu
vegetable	veg
versus	vs
very	vy
vessel	vsl
view	vw
vitamin	vit
vision	vzn
volume	vol
vulnerable	vul

W

we	w
weight	wat
were	wr
west	W
what	wt
where	whr
which	wch
who	wh
why	y
with	wv
without	wvt
wood	wd
would	wld

X

xray	xry

Y

yard	yd
year / yearly	yr / yrly
you	u
you all	y'al
you'd / you would	u'd
your / you're	ur / u'r

Your personal electronic shorthand dictionary may look very different to mine. It depends on the subject of the majority of your note-taking.

If I was in the military, I would probably abbreviate all the ranks (**Lt** = lieutenant, **Gen** = general, etc.). If I was in medicine, I'd use all the medical abbreviations for diseases, procedures, and departments/specialities.

People who are studying find it very useful to go through their textbooks or online workbooks to pick out frequently-used words and phrases. They then make up suitable abbreviations for those.

~ PART THREE ~

Speeding Up

GETTING FASTER

YOU'LL FIND TIPS and tricks in this chapter to get faster in your note-taking. Before you do, though, please take a quick look at the 'How Not To End Up In Pain' chapter again. I can almost hear the groan from here! But it's really important.

There are two ways to get significantly faster:

1. Improve your ***typing speed***
2. Use ***software shortcuts***

The people I have worked with who have made the most impressive results have been the ones who did both! I use both myself. Even though I have a fast typing speed, I still work on it. A few times a week, I'll hop on a typing tutor and practice drills. Numbers were my weakness but I'm okay on those, after a lot of practice – it's symbols I focus on now!

How to improve your typing speed

It's important to be able to touch type. Not having to look at the keyboard when you type will really speed up your electronic note-taking.

There's no shortcut, unfortunately, the only way to learn to touch type is to spend time learning and practicing.

The more you type, the more familiar you will get with the key layout and, in time, your fingers will automatically go where they need to. Muscle memory is a wonderful thing!

There are software packages you can buy that can help, or try TypingWeb, which is a great free resource:

www.typingweb.com

If you don't have regular access to the Internet, it can be hepful to download a program that you can use offline. There is a good one called Type Faster Portable[18] in the PortableApps suite of programs. It's an oldie but a goodie!

The only secret to typing quickly is knowing where the keys are (which is what typing tutors teach) and practice – lots and lots of practice. Many typing tutor programs make practice fun by including games.

[18] http://portableapps.com/news/2010-12-25_-_typefaster_portable_0.4.2

A Word About Speed On Devices

While people can seem to type quickly on devices, they generally don't get as quickly as they could if they were using a full size keyboard. Even today's larger smartphones have tiny keyboards compared to computers and laptops, forcing us to squidge our fingers up at unnatural angles.

That's fine for short note-taking sessions but if you're taking notes for long periods of time, it might be worth investing in an external keyboard. I found a great Bluetooth one on Ebay.

Not only is it better for finger and hand health, it enables you to get to the same speeds on a device that you can attain on a computer.

If you are taking notes directly on a device, try to break up your note-taking sessions and do some simple hand stretches. Even just putting them together, prayer-like, can give them a nice rest.

And don't forget your neck. So many people hunch over their devices, causing the natural curve in their neck to straighten out. This can cause dreadful pain and surprising health problems. Check out chiropractor Dr John Bergman's videos on YouTube if you want to know more on the importance of neck care.

The bottom line is that we need to be very aware that devices can and do cause us to hunch over like bison - and we don't want to stick that way!

Using Word's AutoCorrect Dictionary

AutoCorrect in Word is a useful tool that few people use very much. You may have noticed that Word will sometimes correct a word that you type incorrectly.

If, for example, you type ***inncorrect*** (with two 'n's instead of one), most versions of Word (unless they have been altered) will change it to ***incorrect*** as soon as you hit the spacebar after the 't'.

We can add our electronic shorthand abbreviations into Word's dictionary so that, as we type, they will automatically readjust into full English. This will save you an ***amazing*** amount of time when typing.

Here's how to use AutoCorrect. Click on the FILE (newer versions of Word) or OFFICE link (older versions of Word) at the top left of the Word screen.

Then select **Options** (newer versions) or **Word Options** (older versions). It's on the left side of the screen, usually quite low down.

Choose **Proofing**, then **AutoCorrect Options**:

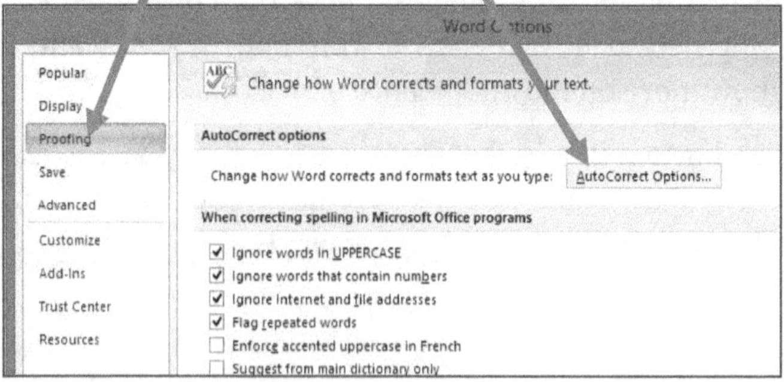

You will see the standard options that Word comes with for AutoCorrect. You can deselect or select these as you wish. What we are concerned with are the tables in the middle and lower part of the window.

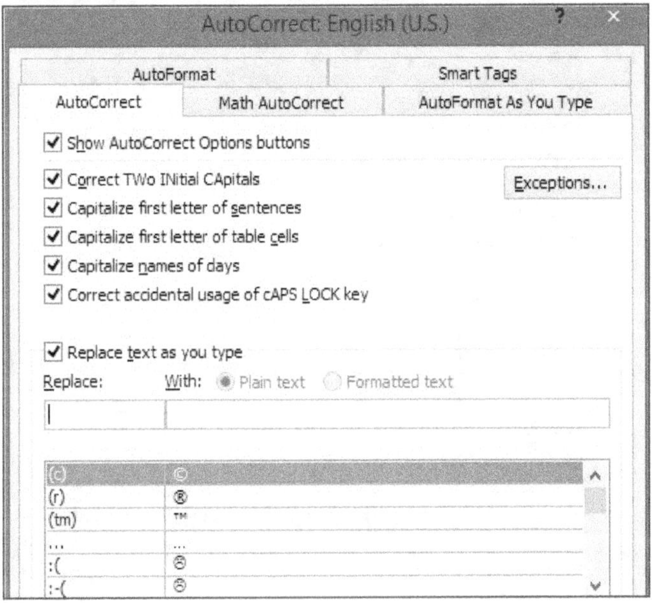

As you can see, Word has added a number of things that will change into symbols. This is like electronic shorthand! When we type a left-hand bracket, followed by a 'c', followed by a right-hand bracket, the word will change into a copyright symbol – ©. Same for a registration mark (®) and the trademark symbol (™).

All we need to do is type in the electronic shorthand abbreviation in the left-hand box and the word we want it to become when it is corrected in the right-hand box.

Here I have added a capital 'O' and told Word that whenever, I type it on its own, I want it to correct to 'only'.

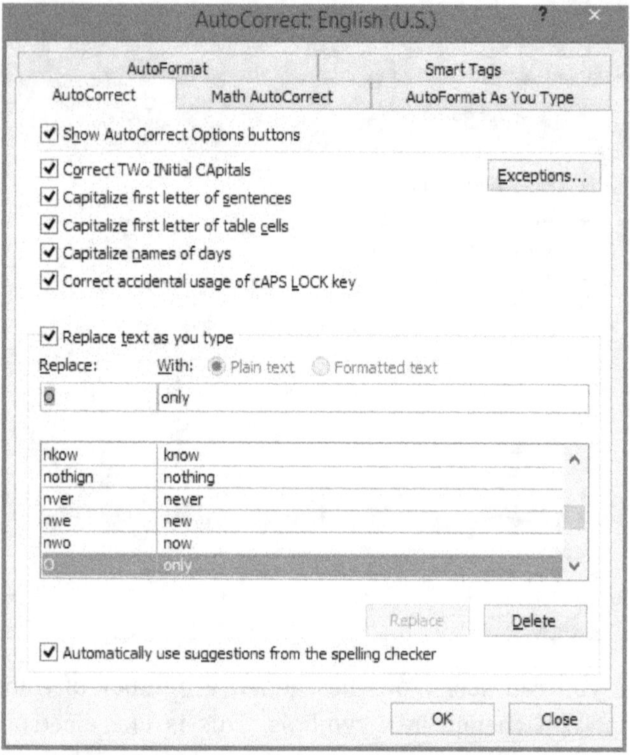

Note that this will only correct a capital 'O' on its own, not a small 'o' on its own (which Word will correct to be a capital 'O' if it is the first word in a sentence) or a capital 'O' if it follows another letter, e.g. 'home'.

You will need to decide whether or not you want words to correct themselves immediately or wait until you run spellchecker. That's up to you. If you prefer to wait until you run spellchecker, just deselect the checkbox 'Replace text as you type' in the AutoCorrect window.

I've added all the words from the Suggested Electronic Shorthand Dictionary chapter to my AutoCorrect dictionary. I didn't do them all at once though.

This is powerful stuff and I've seen people get really carried away, adding everything they can possibly think of to the AutoCorrect database. The trouble is, the usually do it before they get thoroughly used to the shorthand abbreviations themselves and forget what they added!

So I'd advise you to just add a few things that you know you are going to use. Then practice, practice, practice until you get thoroughly used to those shorthand words before adding new ones.

Also, you need to be sure that you only add words that you will **only** use for shorthand. Don't, for example, be tempted to add 'a' as an abbreviation or you won't be able to use it normally again! I've made mistakes like that a few times but it's no big deal, it is easy to remove words from the AutoCorrect database.

Adding AutoCorrect To The Quick Access Toolbar

If it is too fiddly to go via the File/Office button and Word Options to get to the AutoCorrect window every time you want to add or remove a word from the database, you can add AutoCorrect as an option on the toolbar.

Click the little **arrow** on the Quick Access toolbar and choose **More Commands**.

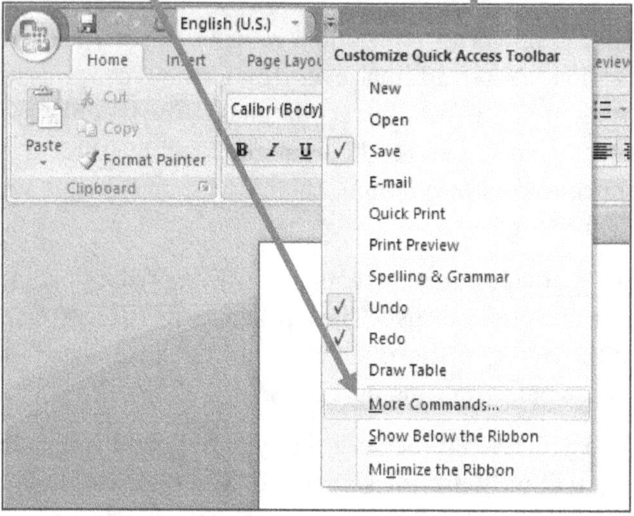

NOTE: Your Quick Access toolbar may be in a different position to mine. It should be either somewhere on the ribbon or at the bottom of the Word screen.

Choose **Commands Not in the Ribbon**:

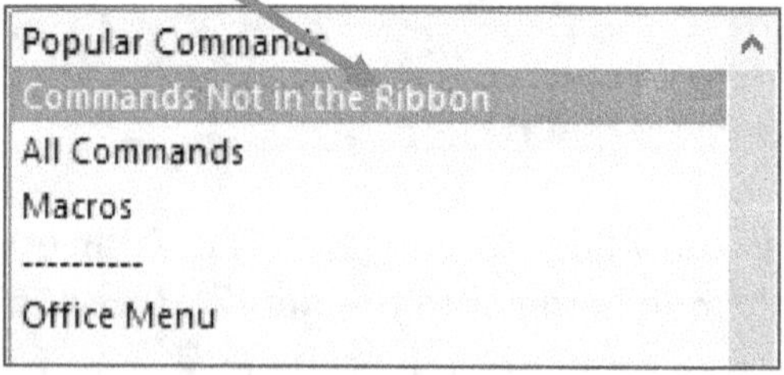

Select **AutoCorrect Options** and click **Add**. It will appear in the right-hand column.

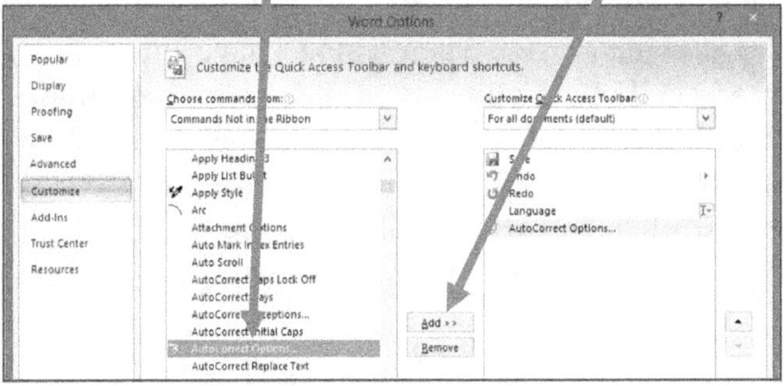

Click **OK** to continue (not shown – bottom-right of window).

The AutoCorrect icon should appear in the QuickAccess Toolbar – it's like a little lightning bolt.

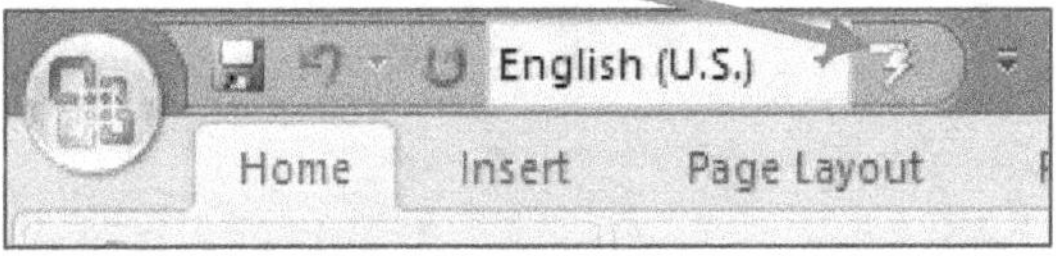

It will make it much easier and quicker to bring up next time you need it.

You can add other commands to the AutoCorrect dictionary. I have several: Insert Page/Section Breaks, Drop Cap Options, Styles, and Mark Entry (for adding words/phrases to an index).

Deleting Words

You may you add a word to the AutoCorrect dictionary, then find it annoying when typing. I have 'int' change to 'interest'. If I type a bit sloppily, I type 'in the' without a space between the words, so it becomes 'interest he'. I considered deleting 'int/'interest' from my dictionary but, as it happens so infrequently, I just use the CTRL + Z combination to undo Word's correction, and carry on.

If you want to take words out, though, it's no problem. In AutoCorrect Options, start typing the word in the left-hand **Replace** box.

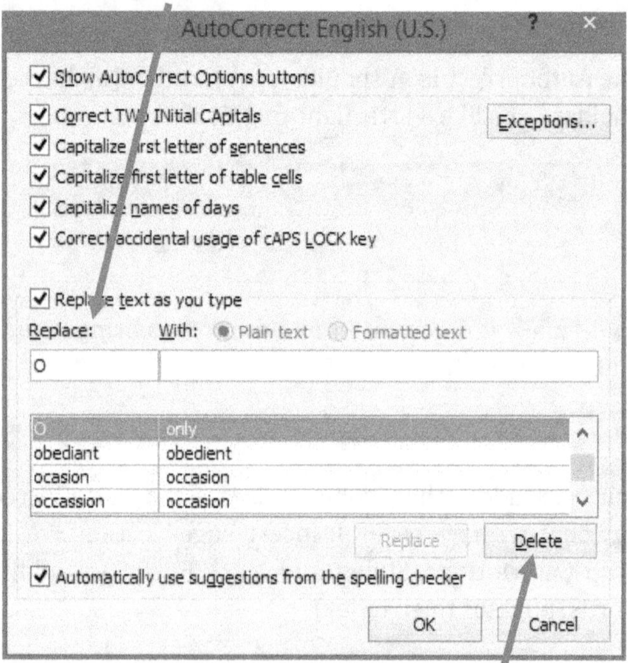

Select the word from the list and click **Delete**. Click OK to close.

WHAT TO DO WITH YOUR NOTES

IN THE OLD days, shorthand notes had to be typed up very soon after taking them. That's because there are a lot of ambiguities with traditional shorthand. You had to type your notes up before you forgot a lot of what they were about! The typing up took up a lot of time.

We are very fortunate now. Whether you take your notes on a device or a computer, it's quick and easy to get them into the format you want and either keep them as they are or change them into full English.

As electronic shorthand can be read back even years after the notes were taken, you don't ***have to*** change your notes to full English. Lots of people keep their notes as they are, in electronic shorthand, stored on their devices and synced to the cloud. Students tend to prefer this method. I have tons of notes on my iPhone, taken during meetings, church services, and training sessions. They are all automatically backed up to iCloud and I also send them to Evernote, where I can tag them and store them in relevant notebooks for easy retrieval later.

For business and other uses, you may need to transfer your notes to a computer and 'upgrade' them to full English in order to share them with others or use them for other purposes. Even though you need to go through to change the electronic shorthand into full English, it is still a whole lot quicker than typing them up manually.

Correcting in Word

AutoCorrect is our friend when we're typing directly into Word. It doesn't work like that when importing text into Word though. If you sync your notes from your device and copy & paste them into a Word document, AutoCorrect won't leap into action and correct everything.

What you need to do is run the spellcheck. Click **Review** on the toolbar on the ribbon, then click **Spelling & Grammar**. The spellcheck will run, giving you the chance to either Ignore or Change words that it flags up.

I suggest chosing CHANGE ALL for your electronic shorthand words as, if you've used a word once in your notes, there will probably be more occurences of it.

I usually do a read-through after running the spellcheck, to pick up on things the spellcheck might not have picked up. Word's spellcheck doesn't flag up single letters – such as **b** for 'be' and **g** for 'go' – so Find & Replace is the best way to deal with them. Run it as you spot letters/words on your read-through that spellcheck didn't pick up.

Here's how:

Click **CTRL** and **H** on the keyboard to bring up the File & Replace window.

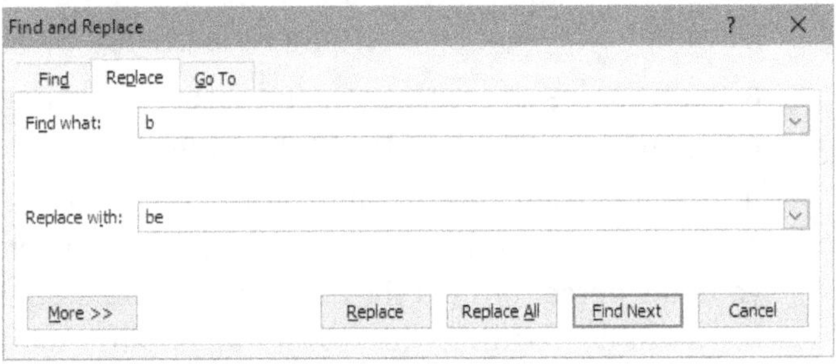

Type in the incorrect word/letter in the **Find what** box and type in the correct word in the **Replace with** box.

Then click **Replace All.**

There are a few tricks to this. I usually do 4 run-throughs of each letter/word. One with no space before it but one after it; one with a space before and a space after it; one with a comma after it (no space) and one with a period after it (no space).

It sounds complicated but it really doesn't take long! It's totally worth it, as it saves a whole lot of time in long documents.

School/College Notes

There are two main ways that note-taking helps with learning.

Firstly, the act of taking notes during a lecture/lesson has multiple effects.

- It keeps you awake and alert. When we are sitting down, we can easily get drowsy. The movement of your hands during your note-taking will keep your brain from switching off – or over to something more interesting! This affects every type of learning style – not just kinesthetic learners.
- It taking helps concentration and focus – meaning that you absorb more of the information.
- It involves the hand-brain connection. You are making new neural pathways in your brain when you take notes through the act of taking something in audibly, writing it down physically, and processing it mentally.

Secondly, the research on note-taking and exam results has shown that what you do with your notes afterwards has a massive effect on how well you remember and understand the topic.

There's a specific system of note-taking that was deviced by a professor, Walter Pauk. It's called the Cornell Note-Taking Method, as he was a professor at Cornell University in the 1950s. He wrote a book, *How To Study In College*, where he teaches his idea. The book is still available on Amazon and elsewhere.

It's very simple. It uses a piece of paper that is split into two columns and one row. The row is at the bottom of the page. The wide right-hand column is for the note-taking, this is the 'Notes' column and is to be used during the class. The narrow left-hand column is to be used after the class. It should be used for condensing the information in the wide column into concise bullet points. This is the 'Cues' column.

The bottom row is for an overall summary of the class, writing down the top/main ideas for quick and easy reference afterwards. This is the 'Summary' row.

It works because you get a double whammy. Not only do you benefit from the act of taking the notes during class, you go back over the notes after the class (preferably within 24hrs, according to Professor Pauk) to summarise them. This helps with the understanding and recall of the topic – especially when it comes to exam time. When revising, it will only take a quick read of the cues and summaries to bring the topic back to mind. It's brilliant.

We can use it in Word by adding a simple table to a document and typing in the right-hand column.

We can use it on a device by taking notes as normal in a note-taking app, then transferring them to a computer and putting them into Word, then summarising them.

There is plenty of advice online about how to use the Cornell Note-Taking Method or you can download a PDF I have prepared here that explains it and also shows how to use tables in Word:

http://www.digitalnotetaking.org/cornellnotetaking

One thing I particularly like about the Cornell Method is that it gets around the usual note-taking advice about not trying to take down every word during a lecture. You don't have to but you can – because you're going to summarize it afterwards.

I do like to take down as much as I can because of the problems with my memory. Unless I write things down, they disappear from my brain. It also helps keep me focused and awake. If I don't take notes, I drift off very quickly!

WRAPUP

HERE'S A QUICK wrapup of everything we've covered.

Lesson One	Leave out short vowels. Keep in long vowels.
Lesson Two	Keep all initial vowels except in special abbreviations. Keep end vowels apart from 'e'.
Lesson Three	Phonetics - write what you hear, not how you know words should be spelled.
Lesson Four	Use abbreviations whenever possible.

Create your own abbreviations and add them to your personal electronic shorthand dictionary.

Utilize capitals – e.g. T = thing, O = only.

Getting Faster

Learn to touch type – practice is the key thing.

Use an external keyboard on a smartphone or tablet for long note-taking sessions.

Keep adding to your electronic shorthand dictionary.

Add to and use the AutoCorrect database in Word – it really speeds up your data entry time.

Typing Up

If typing into Word, add abbreviations into the AutoCorrect dictionary.

If typing on a device, send to a computer and open in Word. Use Find/Replace and Spellchecker to convert electronic shorthand abbreviations into full English.

Note Storage	Use cloud-based software such as Dropbox, Google Drive, iCloud, OneDrive. Send notes to Evernote or OneNote.
Learning/Exams	Use the Cornell Note-Taking Method – take notes in class, then summarize them later.

~ APPENDIX 1 ~

Resources, Apps & Software

I LOVE FREE stuff, so I've included some free resources here. There are some that are worth paying for too! You don't really need anything other than Word or a note-taking app on your smartphone, but you may find some of these extra options useful.

Websites

ABBREVIATION HELP

The website www.abbreviations.com contains an extensive collection of commonly-abbreviated words, as well as less well-known ones. Please don't be tempted to try to learn lots of them at once as it could confuse you and prove difficult to read back in weeks to come! It's best to take on just one or two at a time and thoroughly get used to using them in your daily life before learning more.

ENGLISH RULES

If your grasp of English isn't good, or if school was a long time ago for you, this is an excellent site:

www.myenglishteacher.eu/blog

ADVICE ON NOTE-TAKING

http://www.dartmouth.edu/~acskills/success/notes.html

KEYBOARDS

TABLET KEYBOARDS

Onscreen keyboards on smartphones and tablets can be a bit fiddly. It's very easy to hit a wrong key and not realize. So an external, physical keyboard is very useful. You can get full-sized ones, which men tend to prefer, or foldable, smaller ones which are more portable and easy to carry. They are often Bluetooth-enabled, which means that they can be a bit battery-hungry.

Amazon and Ebay are good places to find them.

The **Sparin Ultra Slim Mini Bluetooth Keyboard** is a good choice. It's large enough to satisfy people who like full-sized keyboards and small enough to be slipped into a bag or purse.

Another good choice is a tablet case that includes a keyboard. They tuck in securely and look great, just making the tablet a little more chunky! They do add weight though.

The **iWerkz Foldable Bluetooth Keyboard** is a nice light option and comes with a protective case that doubles as a stand. It has 44-hour run time, which is excellent.

SMARTPHONE KEYBOARDS

Many of the tablet keyboards will work with smartphones. But there are also some neat smartphone covers that contain external keyboards.

I like the **Hype** range. They are thin and light and generally not battery hungry. They usually come with a lead for charging the keyboard separately.

APPS & SOFTWARE

Apps and software enable you to make or save notes locally as well as in the cloud. That means using a secure area on a company's servers that you can access from anywhere. Having your important notes and documents (as well as photos and other things) backed up to the cloud is immensely useful.

It's also stress-reducing. I turned up to teach advanced Microsoft Excel to a group of managers in a charity. They were high-level people and I had worked on my presentation for days. I had a PowerPoint and workbooks for the delegates saved on my laptop. The tech on duty said I couldn't use my own laptop to hook up to their projector, though, and had to use one of theirs. I didn't have a memory stick and neither did he. No stressy meltdown happened, as I was able to log into my Dropbox account to download my presentation and the workbooks for the participants.

If you take important notes for work, you may experience similar relief if you need to retrieve them quickly or in a different location.

I prefer storing my documents in the cloud, as it is more secure than carrying a memory stick, which could be lost or stolen.

For personal things, too, note-taking and syncing can be a lifesaver. When we get medical news, we can find it hard to take everything in and remember it afterwards. Now, I always take extensive notes when I'm at a medical appointment. It's so handy to be able to retrieve them again at follow-up appointments.

Let's have a look at some of the best apps and programs for note-taking and storage.

IOS

The native IOS Notes app is the most stable of all I have tried. I don't think mine has ever crashed – something I can't say for any other apps! It also has the big advantage of syncing seamlessly with iCloud so, if you take notes on an iPhone or iPad, you can access them on any computer/laptop that has iCloud installed.

ANDROID

The Android smartphones and tablets I have tried haven't come with a native notes app so I'm guessing that most don't. However, there is a wide range of apps you can download – generally free – to try out. I haven't come across one I love yet so I generally use Evernote if I'm using a Droid.

MULTI-PLATFORM

I did a lot of research when writing this book to see which were the most useful popular note-taking apps.

I haven't included apps that I don't use personally as I can't speak for how stable they are. It's incredibly annoying to take notes in an important lecture or meeting and have the app crash part-way through – you're liable to lose a lot of important information.

The two apps that came up most frequently were Evernote and Microsoft's OneNote. What I found was that – perhaps unfairly – many business people favor Evernote and many academics/teachers favor OneNote. As they are so similar – in function if not in aesthetics - it's hard to see why the demarcation exists.

I can recommend both, as I use both for different purposes.

The other services that came up were ones I have used for years – Dropbox and GoogleDrive (formerly GoogleDocs). These now both come as apps but were originally just software for computers. They are both cloud-based. As a habitual library-user, I love this facility. I'm able to access documents that I have on my home computer from anywhere in the world, thanks to my [free] Dropbox account.

Let's have a closer look at each of these...

EVERNOTE

The early versions of Evernote weren't very stable so I tried it and rejected it for note-taking. I didn't go back to it until my friend, author Nancy Hendrickson, wrote a book on how writers can best use it. I found that, over the years, Evernote had made huge improvements and now crashes are much more rare than they used to be.

I use it a lot for research, sending things to Evernote that I discover online and want to read later. I also scan in tons of stuff. All my household and business receipts into it so I can find them easily when it comes to tax time!

I know lots of people who take notes directly into Evernote but I still prefer the native IOS Notes app for direct note-taking if I'm on a device. I take notes in meetings, seminars, and when doing training courses (off and online), which I send to Evernote. A lot of students use it for storing their lecture notes. It's so easy to assign 'tags' to notes – multiple ones if necessary – to make it easy to find them and relate them to similar topics.

OneNote

I was purely an Evernote user until I did an interview with Darrell Webster, a Microsoft expert. He showed me the wonders of OneNote and I was hooked. It is, like Evernote, available both on computers and mobile devices and syncs between them. It is similar in many ways and a great way to upload precious documents and notes to the cloud.

Also like Evernote, it is free. It comes down to personal preference which you choose. I prefer the layout and appearance of Evernote but I know plenty of people who feel the same about OneNote.

Dropbox

I've used Dropbox for about 10 years and can't imagine life without it. It's a small piece of software that sits unobtrusively on your computer and it also comes in app form for devices. Anything you save to Dropbox also saves to the app (which updates every time you open it on the device).

The beauty of Dropbox is that you don't have to do anything, you barely even remember it's there. It syncs in the background and doesn't draw attention to itself.

I use Dropbox for all my documents and images. So, any notes I take or writing that I do on my laptop automatically saves locally (i.e. on the computer) and in the cloud, on Dropbox's servers.

Dropbox files (and folders) can be shared with other Dropbox users. So, if you were working on a project with someone else, you could give them access to a folder that you create for that project.

Dropbox is open source (free) software but you have to pay for more space if you fill the free allocation. If you only use it for documents you would take a long time and a lot of typing to go over the limit. It's photos and videos that tend to fill it up. You can get more space by recommending friends to the service. I built up mine to 20GB by doing that.

GoogleDrive

I used to be a huge GoogleDrive (GDrive) fan until I accidentally locked myself out of my Gmail account when I upgraded my laptop. I get so used to programs remembering passwords for me that I tend to forget them!

I had 2-step verification on, which meant that I had to verify who I was before they would let me reset my password. They wanted to call me or send me a text but I was out of my home country and using a foreign SIM. They wouldn't let me in and wouldn't accept a new telephone number. So I was locked out not only from Gmail but also other Google services – including Gdrive. I abandoned GDrive and stick to Dropbox now.

But the principle of GDrive is the same as Dropbox. It puts a small piece of software on your computer and anything you save to the GDrive folder(s) will be synced to the cloud and accessible from other computers and devices.

It's completely free and very useful if you aren't a password-forgetter like me!

~ APPENDIX 2 ~

Answers To Exercises

Lesson One

1.

Give me your tired, your poor, your huddled masses yearning to breathe free. The wretched refuse of your teeming shore. Send these, the homeless, tempest-tost to me, I lift my lamp beside the golden door.

From *The New Colossus*, a sonnet by Emma Lazarus which is engraved on a bronze plaque inside the Statue of Liberty.

2.

Beautiful dreamer, wake unto me, Starlight and dew drops are waiting for thee; Sounds of the rude world heard in the day, Lull'd by the moonlight, have all pass'd away!

From *Beautiful Dreamer,* a song by Stephen Collins Foster.

3.

Word	Short	Long
Need		x
Shop	x	
Stay		x
Mad	x	
Made		x
Lock	x	

4.

Abbreviated Word	Word in Full	Explanation
wl	will	Say it quickly: 'wl'. It sounds like 'will'. It could be 'wool' but 'wool' has a slightly longer 'ull' sound for most people.

Abbreviated Word	Word in Full	Explanation
wul	wool	The double 'oo' sounds like 'uh'. Say 'wul' and it sounds like 'wool'.
ht	hat / hit / hot	Again, say it quickly and it sounds like any of the words on the left. Within the context of a sentence it should be obvious which word it is.
hat	hate	Say it with the long 'a' and it is obviously 'hate'. We are leaving off the 'e' because it doesn't have a sound in this word.
bled	bleed	Say the long 'eeee' and it can only be 'bleed'.
tak	take	The long 'A' means it has to be 'take'.

Abbreviated Word	Word in Full	Explanation
lok	look	The long 'O' could be 'oh' or 'ooo'. In this case it is 'look'.
gd	God / good	You may not often have to use both in a document but if you do - as I do when taking notes in church - you may want to adopt different abbreviations for each. I use 'gd' for 'God' and 'gud' for 'good. 'gud' could also be 'gude' but I've never had occasion to use that!
metng	meeting	The 'met' part has to be 'meet' and the 'ng' is short for 'ing', which doesn't need the 'i' because it's not a long sound

5.

Abbreviated Word	Word in Full	Explanation
little	ltl	You don't need the 'i' because it's a short vowel. The final 'e' isn't sounded so can be safely left out.
better	btr	This could also be 'butter' or 'batter' but you will be able to tell from the rest of the sentence. Unless it's a recipe!
handsome	hnsm	You don't need the 'a' or 'o' because they are short sounds. The 'd' isn't sounded by most people and the final 'e' is hardly ever needed.

pretty	prty	An easy one. Could also be party but you will be able to tell by the rest of the sentence. When a consonant is doubled, as the 't' is here or the 'l is in 'full', and the second letter is silent, you don't need both.
beep	bep	Doubled vowels, as doubled consonants, are hardly ever needed in Speedwriting. Say the 'e' as a long vowel and it sounds like 'eee' so beeep.

6.

Jonny Be Good
Good Vibrations
Respect
Smells Like Teen Spirit

Lesson Two

1.

Th alrm rng erly @ th zu

=

The alarm rang early at the zoo

2.

Jak th gko is blu

=

Jake the gecko is blue

3.

An apl ech dy kps the doc away

=

An apple a day keeps the doctor away

4.

Th ew at th pza

=

The ewe ate the pizza

Now write out the electronic shorthand for the following.

5.

Oh, Danny Boy, the pipes, the pipes are calling from glen to glen, and down the mountain side

=

Oh Dnny By, th pips, th pips, r calg frm gln 2 gln, & dwn the mwntn sid.

From *Oh, Danny Boy,* ballad written by Frederic Weatherley to the *Londonderry Air* tune.

Nothing too odd here. Notice that I didn't use **O** represent 'oh' – that's because I use a capital O for 'only'.

Dnny - this is a case where duplicate consontants are sometimes necessary. If 'Danny' was spelled 'Dany' it would be pronounced DANE-y.

Mwntn for 'mountain' is a useful one. W can represent the 'ow' sound in lots of words.

Lesson Three

1.

My drtr's dns s gd enuf

=

My daughter's dance is good enough

2.

Dd u rit th crd & rp th prznt?

=

Did you write the card and wrap the present?

3.

Uz th nif in ur rit hnd

=

Use the knife in your right hand

4.

Th gsts at th htl thrt th nu sin ws lvly

=

The guests at the hotel thought the new sign was lovely

5.

Call me crazy, but I love you

=

cal m krz, bt I lv u

'm' is a good abbreviation for 'me'.

krz is an odd one – probably not one you'll use very often. It reads back as 'craze' but in context it is clear that it means 'crazy'.

6.

Singing hymns on the island

=

sngg hms on th ilnd

I often use just 'g' instead of 'ing', which is why 'singing' became **sngg**. If you prefer, you could add the 'n' – **sngng**.

7.

Your handkerchief is in the wash

=

ur hnkrchf is in the wsh

'Handkerchief' doesn't need any vowels as it is a long word, so it's obvious what it is without them.

8.

I have a cough and a cold

=

i hv a cf & a cld

A nice easy one!

Lesson Four

1.

f u g 2 th c, t s cld

=.

If you go to the sea, it is cold

2.

t s imp 2 g strat acrs

=

It is important to go straight across

3.

ps m th 2x4 blk

=

Pass me the two by four block

4.

the cst s $1K

=

The cost is $1,000 (or one thousand dollars)

5.

any1 els bt u

=

Anyone else but you

6.

sh wrks hrd 4 th $

=

She works hard for the money

7.

f th % v ppl @ th evnt s sml, u wl nt mak enuf $

=

If the percentage of people at the event is small, you will not make enough money

8.

th ptnts BP s > 150 so h nds a Px & an inj

=

The patient's blood pressure is greater than 150 so he needs a prescription and an injection

9.

th liq ws M-us

=

The liquid was multi-use

10.

Th 5 ppl n th tp % v th cls al cam frm th sam C

=

The five people in the top percentage of the class all came from the same country

11.

Moneywise is another very different multinational company

=

$wz s another vy dif Mnl co

12.

The difference between carbon monoxide and carbon dioxide is small but very important

=

the difr bet CO and CO2 s sml bt vy imp

Difr is a useful abbreviation for 'difference' if you use 'dif'for 'different. I also use 'dift' for 'difficult'.

'bet' is a great abbreviation of 'between' but if you use 'beat' a lot in your note-taking, you may prefer to use 'btwn' for 'between'.

If I didn't know the chemical symbols, I would have used **carbn monox** and **carbn diox**.

13.

Government cutbacks caused demonstrations in the streets

=

gov ctbks czd demos n th strets

gov is a common abbreviation for 'government'.

Ctbks is obvious.

I love using Z in words – it cuts out 3 letters here in 'caused'.

strets might seen unnecessary as **strts** would do but I use that for 'starts'. I could write 'streets' as **st.s** but it's not a word I use very often so I haven't made a very cut-down abbreviation to add to my dictionary.

14.

Problems arose when the number of tickets sold was greater than the number of seats available

=

probs arz wn th # v tkts sld ws > th # v sets avlbl

This is a great sentence for cutting letters out!

All fairly easy I hope. You may not have thought of them when typing it out yourself but, now you've seen my version, some of them may come to mind in future.

Extra Exercises

1.

Pride relates more to our opinion of ourselves; vanity to what we would have others think of us.

2.

All happy families are alike; each unhappy family is unhappy in its own way.

3.

It was a queer, sultry summer, the summer they electrocuted the Rosenbergs, and I didn't know what I was doing in New York.

4.

In the late summer of that year we lived in a house in a village that looked across the river and the plane to the mountains.

5.

Shall I compare thee to a summer's day?
Thou art more lovely and more temperate.

6.

Like as the waves make towards the pebbled shore,
so do our minutes hasten to their end,
each changing place with that which goes before,
in sequent toil all forwards do content.

7.

You will rejoice to hear that no disaster has accompanied the commencement of an enterprise which you have regarded with such evil forebodings.

8.

Mr Hungerton, her father, really was the most tactless person upon earth.

9.

The year 1866 was signalised by a remarkable incident, a mysterious and puzzling phenomenon, which doubtless no-one has yet forgotten.

Lines from the Bible

10.

In the beginning, God creatd the heavens and the earth.

11.

The heavens declare the glory of God.

12.

For I know the plans I have for you, declares the Lord. Plans to prosper you and not to harm you, plans to give you hope and a future.

13.

I can do all things through Christ who strengthens me.

Lines from famous speeches

14.

I have a dream that one day this nation will rise up and live out the true meaning of its creed: "We hold these truths to be self-evident: that all men are created equal."
Martin Luther King

15.

Ask not what your country can do for you, ask what you can do for your country.
J.F. Kennedy

16.

I keep my ideals, because in spite of everything I still believe that people are really good at heart.
Anne Frank

17.

That government of the people, by the people, for the people, shall not perish frim the earth.
Abraham Lincoln, Gettysburg Address

18.

Never in the field of human conflict was so much owed by so many to so few.
Winston Churchill

19.

We shall defend our island, whatever the cost may be. We shall fight on the beaches, we shall fight on the landung grounds, we shall fight in the fields and in the streets, we shall fight on the hills; we shall never surrender.
Winston Churchill

20.

Friends, Romans, countrymen, lend me your ears.
Shakespeare

21.

For fools rush in where angels fear to tread.
Alexander Pope

22.

Fortune favors the bold.
Virgil

23.

Dream as if you'll live forever, live as if you'll die tomorrow.
James Dean

24.

Never doubt that a small group of thoughtful, committed citizens can change the world. Indeed, it is the only thing that ever has.
Margaret Mead

Quotes from politicians

25.

I am not a crook. I have earned everything I have got.
Richard Nixon

26.

The only thing we have to fear is fear itslf.
Franklin Delano Roosevelt

27.

Political leaders still think things can be done through force, but that can't solve terrorism. Backwardness is the breeding ground of terror, and that is what we have to fight.
Mikhail Gorbachev

28.

It is easy to make promises – it is hard work to keep them.
Boris Johnson

29.

There are no disasters, only opportunities. And, indeed, opportunities for fresh disasters.
Boris Johnson

30.

Like Indiana Jones, I don't like snakes – though that might lead some to ask why I'm in politics.
Theresa May

ABOUT THE AUTHOR

LIKE MANY AUTHORS, Michelle has had a number of careers (advertising, public relations, teaching, training). She prefers to put about the idea that this has brought a wealth of experience to her writing rather than the fact that she is a bit fickle.

She devised her own version of electronic shorthand in response to requests from students and colleagues who needed to take notes on their smartphones or computers.

She wrote and developed courses and articles for other people for many years before plucking up the courage to enter the publishing arena herself. She published the first book under her own name in 2012.

Her books include:

- *7 Myths About Aquaponics* (as Michelle Booth)
- *Goodreads for Authors*
- *Inversion Therapy* (as Mia Campbell)
- *How to Index a Book in Word* (publishing Winter 2016)
- *Make Your Book Work Harder* (with Nancy Hendrickson)
- *Mo: The Talking Dog* (as Michelle Booth)
- *PR for Authors*
- *The 10-Day Colon Cleansing Detox* (as Mia Campbell, publishing January 2017)
- *The 10-Day Skin Brushing Detox* (as Mia Campbell)
- *Why Henry VIII Got Fat* (as Mia Campbell)

She also has online courses available on Udemy & other online learning platforms:

- Email Marketing for Authors
- Goodreads for Authors : Book promotion & marketing
- How to create an eBook using open-source software
- Learn how to get your book on CreateSpace
- Electronic Shorthand (the course that this book is based on)

Michelle is from the north-western U.K. and is currently on an extended roadtrip around North America in an RV.

INDEX

H

L

M

N

O

P

R

S

T

V

W

www.ingramcontent.com/pod-product-compliance
Lightning Source LLC
Chambersburg PA
CBHW070319190526
45169CB00005B/1673